THE USBORNE ROUND THE WORLD SONGBOOK

Emma Danes

Designed by Kathy Ward

Illustrated by Radhi Parekh

Songs selected by Sylvestre Balazard and Emma Danes

Music arrangements by Sylvestre Balazard and Anthony Marks

Series editor: Anthony Marks

Language consultants:
Pepe Arti, Joanne Atkinson (School of Oriental and African Studies), Isabel Barbosa, Beate Bowler, Miki Clibbon, Dipali Ghosh, Giovanni Guarnieri, Dr Rosaleen Howard-Malverde (Institute of Latin American Studies), Liu Hongbin, Gaenor Howells, Joyce Jenkins (Japanese Language Association), Esther Jessop, Dr Kim, Esther Lecumberri, Dongill Lee, Sophia Németh, Marta Nuñez, Bisi Ogunbadejo, Dr M. Osman, John Pawson, Konstantia Phoca, Maria Luisa Ramos, Rosette Rozenberg, Christian Sévigny, Carole Shaw, Mrs A. Taiwo, Paul Vincent

With thanks to: Nicole Irving, Sophy Tahta, Kathy Gemmell, Andrew Jones, Katie Elliott, Ulrike zur Nieden, Mita Parekh, Prins Willem Alexander School (Woking), Jim Ferguson (Latin American Bureau)

Contents

India	Flute song: *Khamma mara Nandajinam Lal*	4
USA	If you're happy and you know it	6
Greece	There is the ring: *Nato to dachtilidi*	7
Russia	Kalinka	8
Finland	Is it suddenly now summer?: *No onkos tullut kesä?*	10
France	On the bridge at Avignon: *Sur le pont d'Avignon*	11
Jamaica	Water come a me eye	12
Brazil	Circle song: *Ciranda*	14
Korea	Arirang	15
Mexico	The little beetle: *La cucaracha*	16
Ireland	Cut the loaf	18
Israel	Let's all rejoice: *Hava nagila*	19
Germany	Little Hans: *Hänschen klein*	20
Canada	The clear fountain: *A la claire fontaine*	22
Java	Snaky serpent song: *Ular naga*	23
Scotland	O where, tell me where	24
Spain	Cuckoo, cuckoo: *Cucú, cucú*	26
Wales	There is Daddy: *Dacw Dadi'n mynd i'r ffair*	28
Holland	Little Short Coat: *Altijd is Kortjakje ziek*	29
New Zealand	Greetings to you all!: *Tena ra koutou katoa!*	30
Philippines	Fishing song: *Si nanay, si tatay*	32
South Africa	Lord bless Africa: *Nkosi Sikelel' iAfrika*	33
England	Golden slumbers	34
Japan	Cherry blooms: *Sakura*	36
Hungary	When the spring comes: *Tavaszi szél vizet áraszt*	37
China	Flower drum song: *Hua gu ge*	38
Saudi Arabia	Indian calico: *Bafta hindi*	40
West Indies	Tinga Layo	41
Australia	Kookaburra	42
Italy	Go to sleep: *Ninna nanna*	44
Nigeria	On a farm I saw a bird: *Mo ri eye kan loko*	45
Peru	Please don't forget me: *Ama qonqawaychu*	46

Introduction

The songs in this book are in 24 different languages. They come from over 30 countries around the world, which are shown on the map below. You can sing each song in its original language, or in an English version specially written for this book.

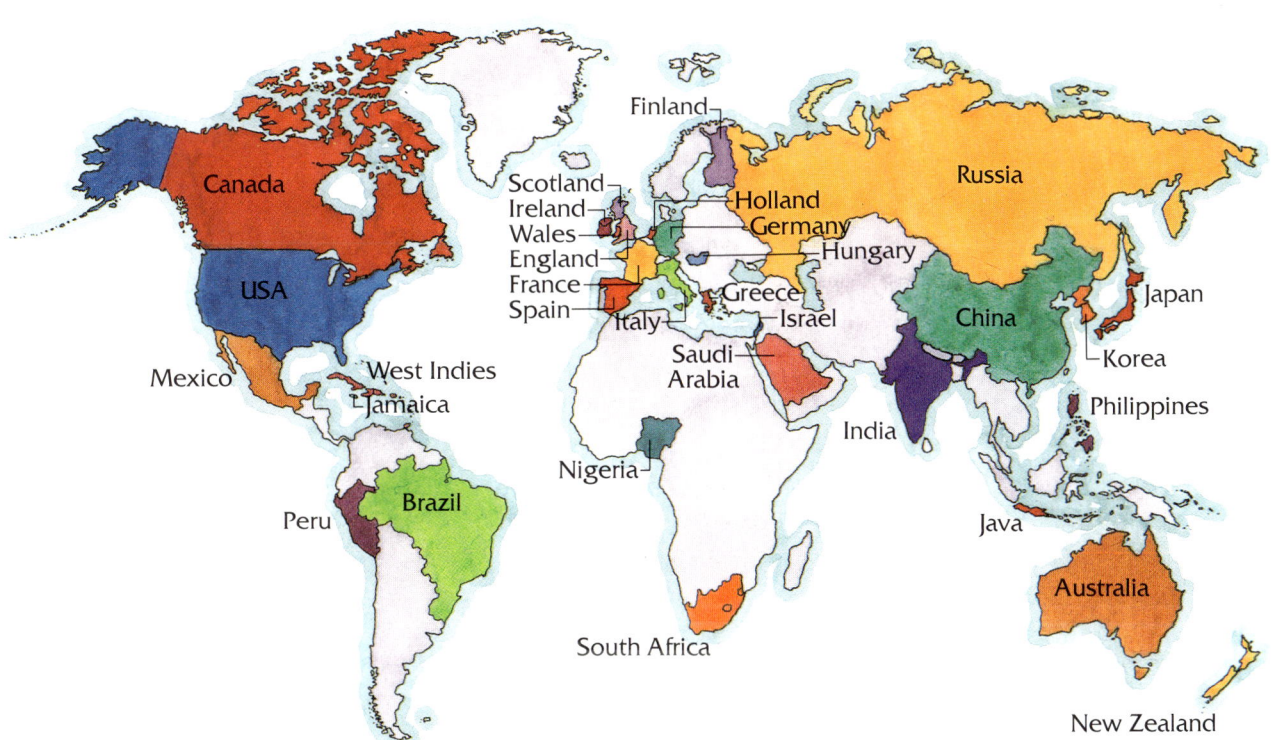

The first verse of each song is written in the music. Usually there are three lines of words. The top line is the English version. The middle line contains the words written in the original language. (Words in languages that use a different system of writing, such as Chinese, have been written out using our alphabet.) The bottom line, in smaller letters, is a guide to help you pronounce the middle line. Read this as though you were reading English words.

Some of the songs have extra verses, shown below the music or on the opposite page. These are written first in English, and then in the original language with a pronunciation guide.

Most of the songs have guitar chords above the music, and there are also tips about using other instruments to accompany your singing. On page 48 there is a chart explaining how to play the guitar chords and an index of the countries in the book.

INDIA

This song is about a milkmaid who is charmed by the god Krishna. The first six measures are a chorus. Sing this twice between each verse, and twice at the end, once with the accompaniment and once without.

Flute song: *Khamma mara Nandajinam Lal*

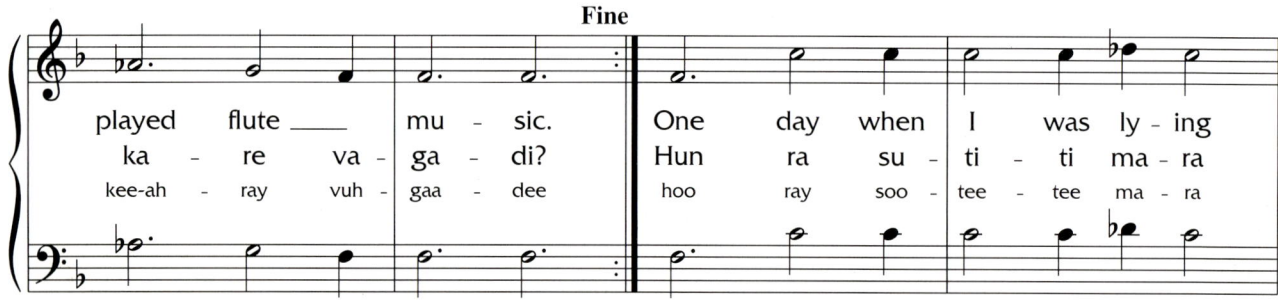

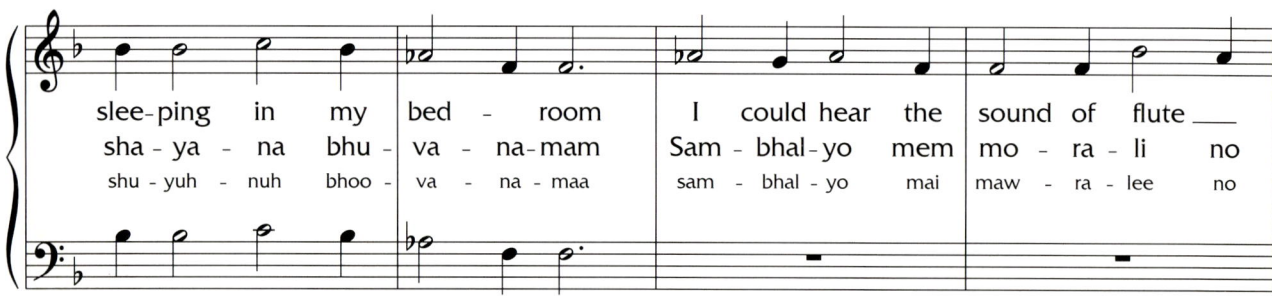

D.C. al Fine

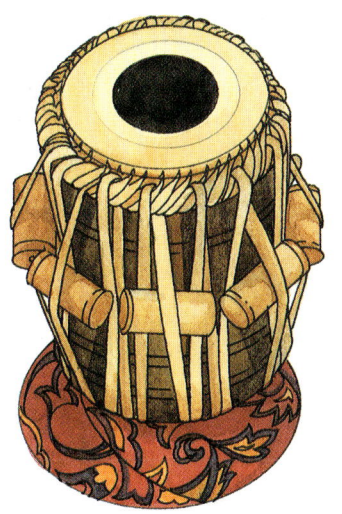

This is a wooden tabla drum.

The sitar is a type of Indian stringed instrument.

This man is playing a pair of drums called tabla. One drum is made of wood, the other of metal. They are resting on cushions.

Said I'd fetch water but I went to see my sweetheart
There I saw the son of Nandaji.
Tell me why you played flute music.

Panida ne bahane jivan jovane hali
pa-nee-da nay buh-ha-nay jee-van jo-va-nay ha-lee
Ditha mem to Nandajinam Lal.
dee-ta mai toh nan-da-jee-na laal
Morali kare vagadi?
maw-ra-lee kee-ah-ray vuh-gaa-dee

I left the water pitcher by the flowing river
I sat on a swing beneath a tree.
Tell me why you played flute music.

Beda melya che mem to sarovara pale
bay-da may-lya chai mai toh sar-o-vuh-ruh par-lay
Hindoli ambani dal.
hin-doe-lee aam-ba-nee daal
Morali kare vagadi?
maw-ra-lee kee-ah-ray vuh-gaa-dee

This is a metal tabla drum.

The type of dance below tells a story. It has many complicated movements for the dancer's feet, body, hands and face.

These dancers are telling the story of Krishna playing his flute.

The dance shown on the right is often performed with the song on the opposite page.

USA

This is an action song. In the first verse, clap your hands twice in the rests in measures 2, 4 and 8. In the other verses you tap your feet or nod your head in the rests. Make the dotted rhythms sound very lively and bouncy.

If you're happy and you know it

If you're hap-py and you know it, clap your hands. If you're

hap-py and you know it, clap your hands. If you're hap-py and you know it, Then your

face will sure-ly show it. If you're hap-py and you know it, clap your hands.

If you're happy and you know it, tap your toe.
If you're happy and you know it, tap your toe.
If you're happy and you know it,
Then your face will surely show it.
If you're happy and you know it, tap your toe.

If you're happy and you know it, nod your head.
If you're happy and you know it, nod your head.
If you're happy and you know it,
Then your face will surely show it.
If you're happy and you know it, nod your head.

Banjos became popular in America in the 19th century.

The first electric guitar was made in America.

GREECE

This song is part of a game. The leader hides a ring in one hand and moves around the singers, pretending to pass it on. One of the other players has to guess who the leader has passed it to.

There is the ring: *Nato to dachtilidi*

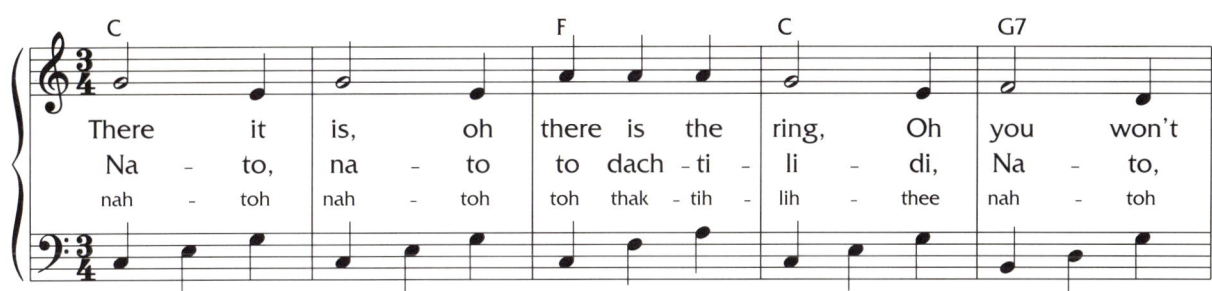
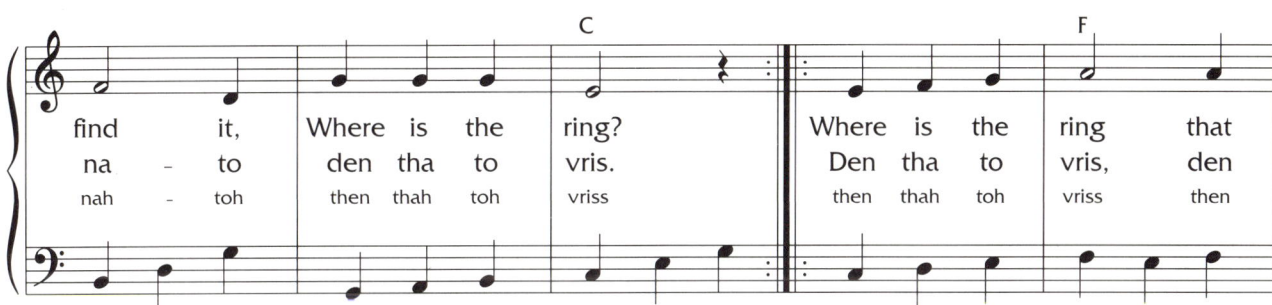

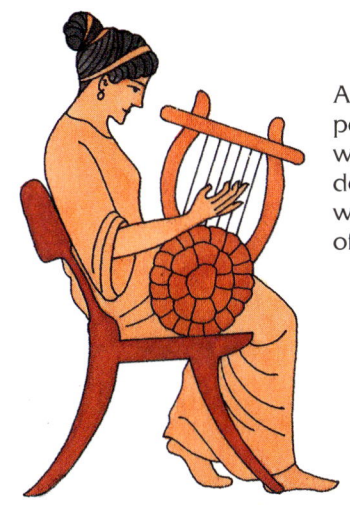

Ancient Greek pots and vases were often decorated with paintings of musicians.

This instrument, called a lyre, was popular in Greece around three thousand years ago.

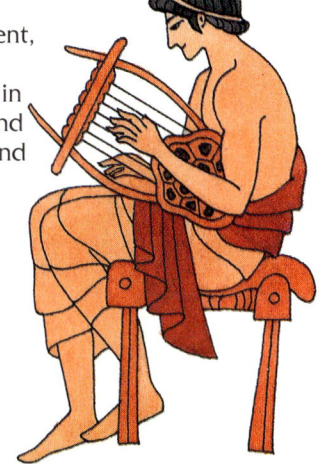

In Greece today, musicians often play bouzoukis (similar to guitars).

RUSSIA

The first eight measures of this song are a chorus. Sing them with the same words before each verse, and again at the end of the song. Sing the song gently and not too fast. You can make the notes with the pause signs (⌢) above them fairly long.

Kalinka

Ka - lin - ka, ka - lin - ka, my lit - tle tree, You are stan - ding in the
Ka - lin - ka, ka - lin - ka, ka - lin - ka mo - ia, Vsa - du ia - go - da ma -
kah - leen - kah kah - leen - kah kah - leen - kah ma - ya fsah - doo ya - guh - da mah -

gar - den with ber - ries for me. Ka - me. Oh! un - der - neath the
- lin - ka, ma - lin - ka mo - ia. Ka - ia. Akh! pod - sos -
- leen - kah mah - leen - kah ma - ya kah - ya akhh pad - sas -

pine tree, un - der - neath the green leaves, You lay me down to
- noi - u, pod zel - en - oi - u, Spat po - lo zhit - e
- noi - oo pad zel - en - oi - oo spaht pa - la zheet - yeh

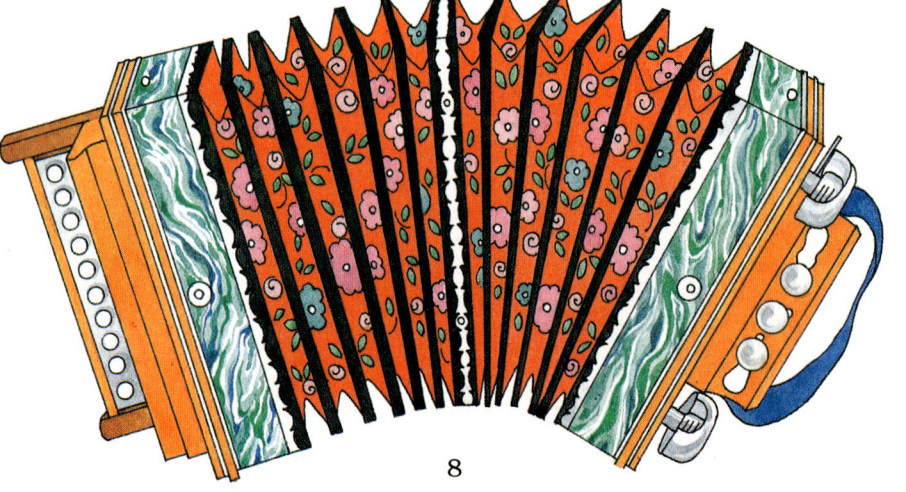

This decorated accordion comes from Russia. You play it by squeezing the bellows in and out.

You press the silver buttons on the left-hand side to play different notes. The buttons on the right change the sounds.

Dancers wear these bell bracelets which make a jingling sound as they move.

Both these instruments are types of clappers. They have several flaps tied together which you shake to make a clacking sound.

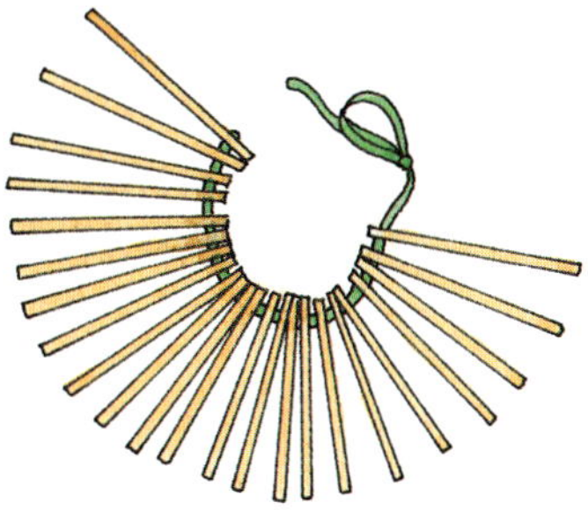

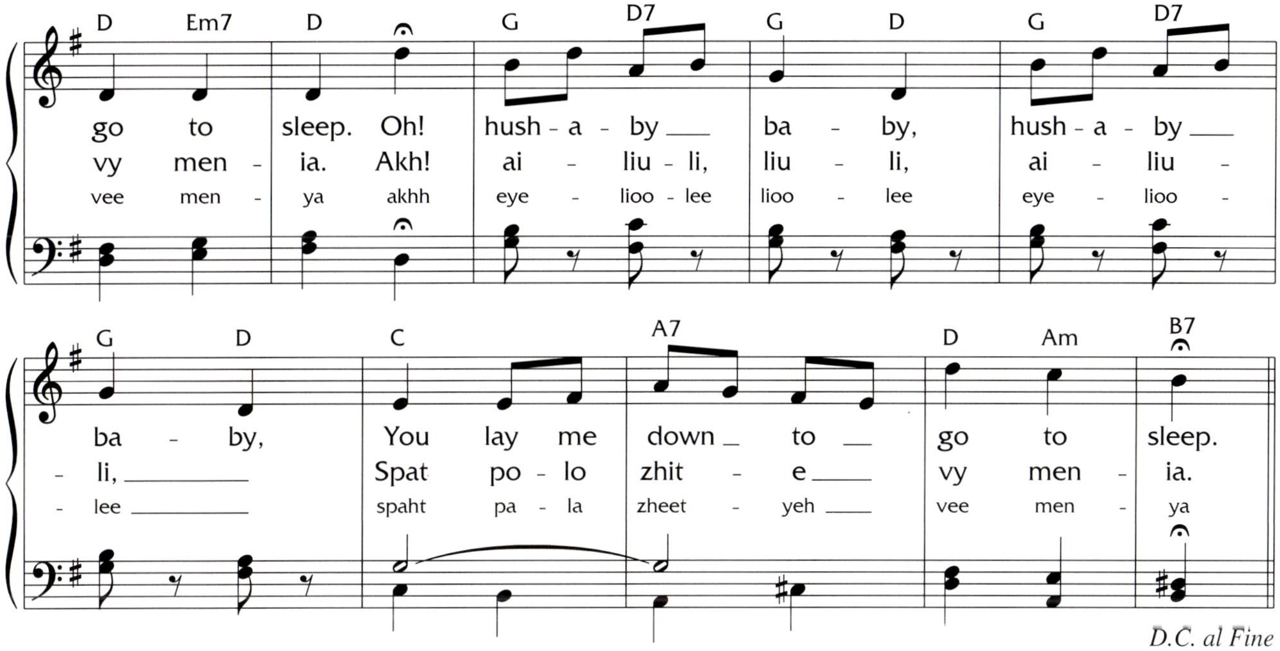

D	Em7	D	G	D7	G	D	G D7

go to sleep. Oh! hush-a-by ____ ba - by, hush-a-by ____
vy men - ia. Akh! ai - liu - li, liu - li, ai - liu
vee men - ya akhh eye - lioo - lee lioo - lee eye - lioo

G	D	C	A7	D	Am	B7

ba - by, _____ You lay me down __ to __ go to sleep.
- li, _____ Spat po - lo zhit - e ____ vy men - ia.
- lee _____ spaht pa - la zheet - yeh ____ vee men - ya

D.C. al Fine

The balalaika is often used in Russia for accompanying songs and dances. It is similar to a guitar, but only has three strings.

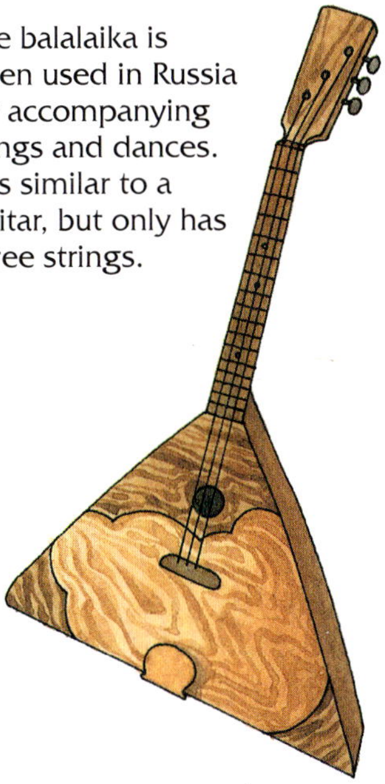

Oh! little green neighbor, little green neighbor,
Don't make a sound above my head.
Oh! hushaby baby, hushaby baby,
Don't make a sound above my head.

Akh! sosenushka ty zelenaia,
akhh sas-yon-oosh-kah tee zel-yon-a-ya
Ne shumi zhe nado mnoi.
ne shoo-mi zhe na-da mnoy
Akh! ai-liuli, liuli, ai-liuli,
akhh eye lioo-lee lioo-lee eye lioo-lee
Ne shumi zhe nado mnoi.
ne shoo-mi zhe na-da mnoy

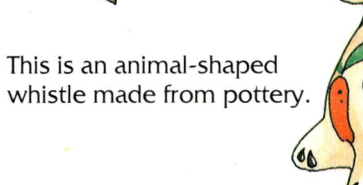

This is an animal-shaped whistle made from pottery.

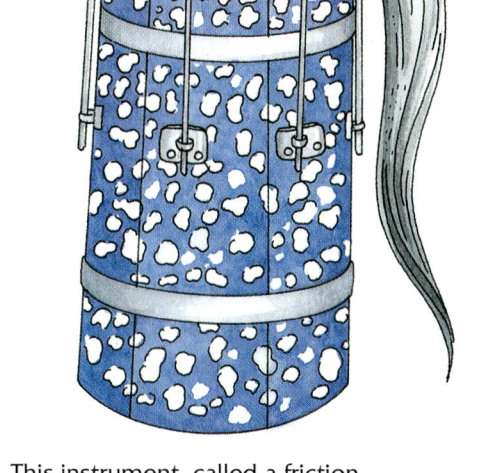

This instrument, called a friction drum, is played by rubbing horsehair through a hole in the skin at the top.

FINLAND

This Christmas song was written a long time ago, but it is still very popular today. Most children in Finland learn to sing it when they are very young. Remember you can check how to play any unfamiliar guitar chords on page 48.

Is it suddenly now summer?: *No onkos tullut kesä?*

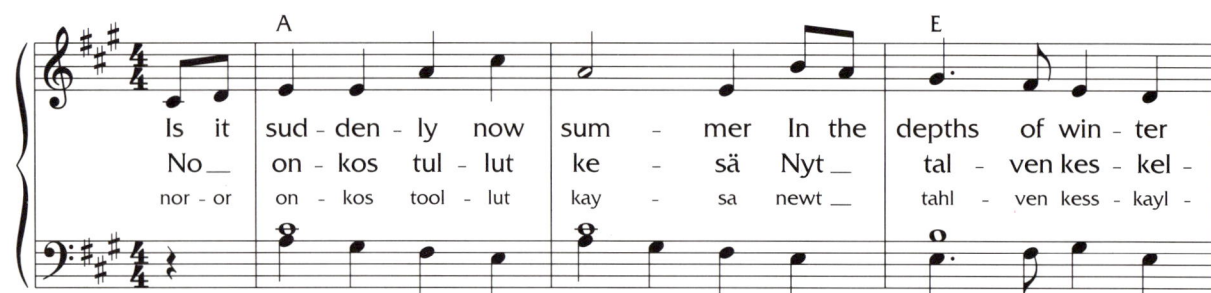

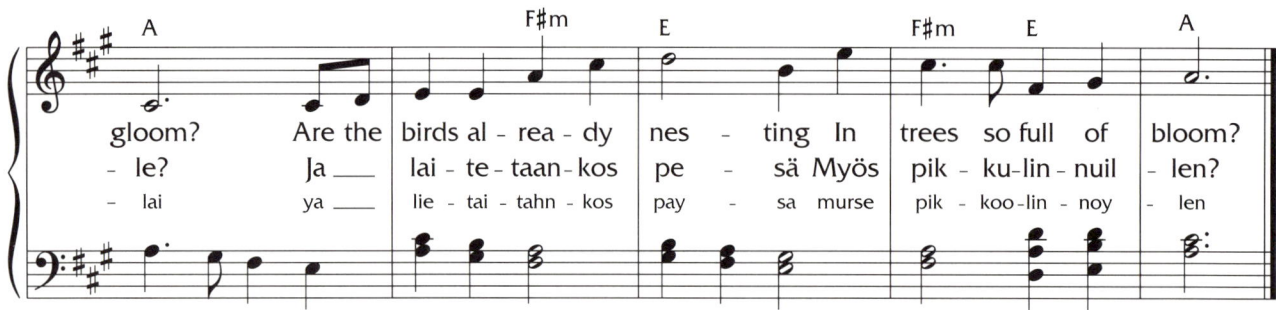

The spruce seems full of blossom
As the candles twinkle bright,
We feel so glad and cheerful
This dark and wintry night.

So cozy, warm and tender
Is how we are feeling here.
Why can't it last forever,
Our Christmas and good cheer?

Jo kuusi kynttilöitä
yoh koo-see kewn-tih-loee-ta
On käynyt kukkimaan,
on kao-newt kook-ee-mahn
Pimeitä talven öitä
pee-mai-ta tahl-ven oee-ta
Näin ehkä valaistaan.
naieen ekhh-kah val-eye-stahn

Ja hyvä, lämmin, hellä
ya hew-va lam-min hel-la
On mieli jokaisen,
on mear-lih yo-kai-sen
Oi jospa ihmisellä
oy yos-pah ikhh-mee-say-la
Ois joulu ainainen!
oys yo-loo eye-ny-nen

This is a shepherd's horn made from tree bark twisted in a spiral.

You hold a jouhikko through the hole at the top and play it with a bow.

This horn has finger holes so you can play different notes.

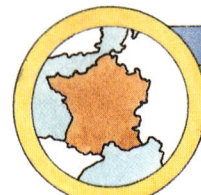

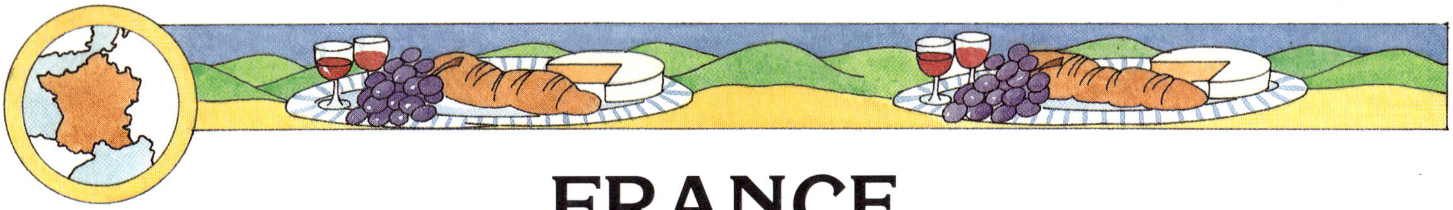

FRANCE

This song is sometimes used for a party game. You can try this for yourself. In the first two lines, skip around in a large circle. Then in measures 9, 10 and 11 the boys bow to the girls. In the next three measures, the girls curtsy to the boys. Sing these measures more slowly.

On the bridge at Avignon: *Sur le pont d'Avignon*

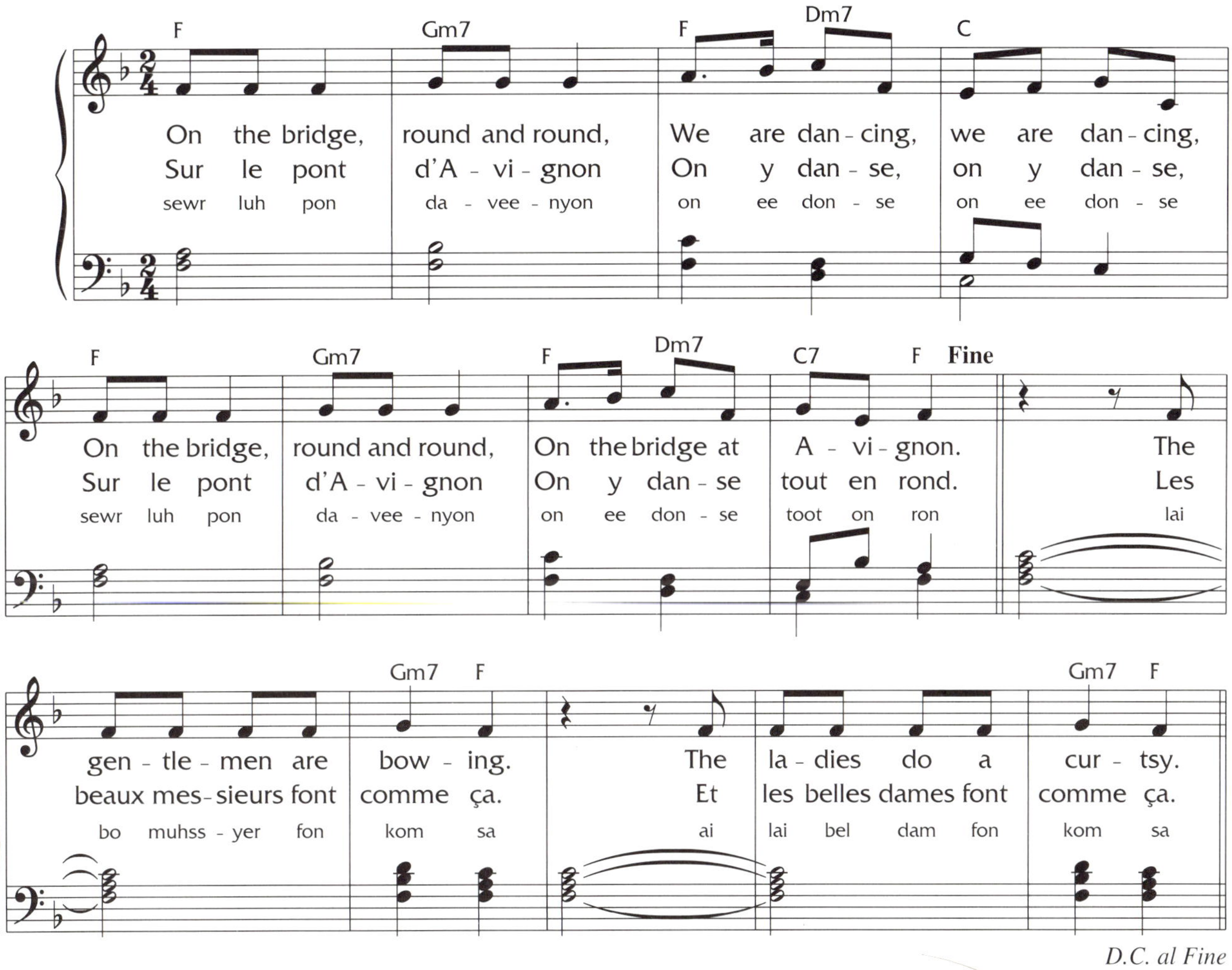
F Gm7 F Dm7 C
On the bridge, round and round, We are dan - cing, we are dan - cing,
Sur le pont d'A - vi - gnon On y dan - se, on y dan - se,
sewr luh pon da - vee - nyon on ee don - se on ee don - se
F Gm7 F Dm7 C7 F Fine
On the bridge, round and round, On the bridge at A - vi - gnon. The
Sur le pont d'A - vi - gnon On y dan - se tout en rond. Les
sewr luh pon da - vee - nyon on ee don - se toot on ron lai
Gm7 F Gm7 F
gen - tle - men are bow - ing. The la - dies do a cur - tsy.
beaux mes - sieurs font comme ça. Et les belles dames font comme ça.
bo muhss - yer fon kom sa ai lai bel dam fon kom sa
D.C. al Fine

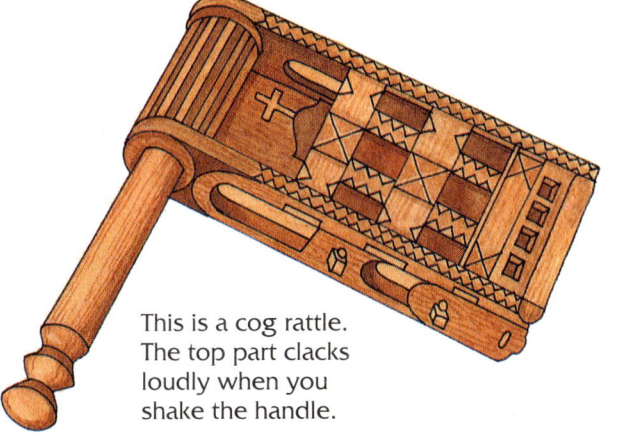

This is a cog rattle. The top part clacks loudly when you shake the handle.

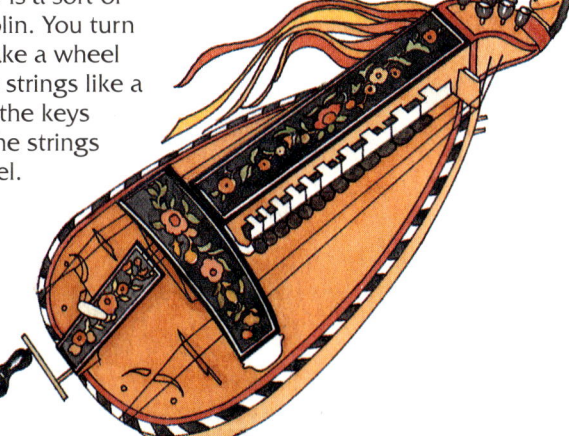

A hurdy-gurdy is a sort of mechanical violin. You turn a handle to make a wheel move over the strings like a bow. Pressing the keys down makes the strings touch the wheel.

JAMAICA

In Jamaica, songs are often accompanied by lots of percussion instruments. You could try playing drums or shakers when you sing this song, using the rhythm in the left-hand piano part. This might seem a bit tricky at first, but it makes the music sound interesting.

Water come a me eye

Ev-'ry time I think of Li-za, Wa-ter come a me eye,

Ev-'ry time I think of Li-za, Wa-ter come a me eye.

Come back, Li-za, come back girl, Wa-ter come a me eye,

Come back, Li-za, come back girl, Wa-ter come a me eye.

Here are some of the percussion instruments which are used in Jamaican music.

A guiro is a hollow wooden instrument with lots of ridges. You scrape it with a stick. This makes a dry, rasping sound.

Congas are tall drums which you usually play with your fingers or the palms of your hands.

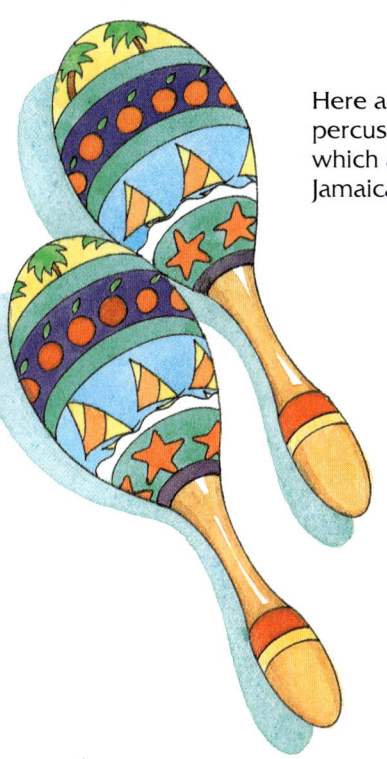

Don't know why you went away,
Water come a me eye.
When you comin' home to stay?
Water come a me eye.
Come back, Liza, come back girl,
Water come a me eye.
Come back, Liza, come back girl,
Water come a me eye.

Maracas have a hollow case filled with seeds or beads which rattle when you shake them.

Steel pans are metal drums which are often played in bands. The tops are divided into separate sections. Each section makes a different note when you hit it.

Larger pans accompany the tunes. They play lower notes, and help to make a strong rhythm.

Soprano (or ping pong) pans are the smallest pans. They usually play 25 different notes, and are used to play the tunes in a band.

There are often other drums and percussion instruments in steel bands, as well as the pans.

BRAZIL

This is a popular children's song in Brazil. Try dancing around in a circle while you sing it, changing direction halfway through the sixth measure. Make the music sound energetic, but do not sing it too fast.

Circle song: *Ciranda*

A ring a ring of ro-ses, Let's all dance a-round to-day. Let's dance round in a cir-cle, Then go back the oth-er way.

Ci-ran-da ci-ran-di-nha, Va-mos to-dos ci-ran-dar. Va-mos dar a me-ia vol-ta, Vol-ta'e me-ia va-mos dar.

see-ran-dah see-ran-deen-ya vah-moos toe-dos see-ran-dahr vah-moos dahr ah may-ah vol-tah vol-tah-eh may-ah vah-moos dahr

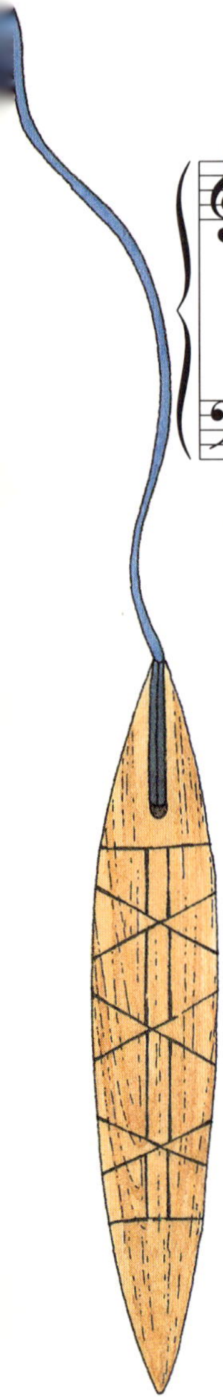

This instrument from Brazil is called a bull-roarer. It makes a sound when you whirl it around in the air. The sound gets higher or lower depending on how fast it is moving.

Musical bows are played in parts of Brazil. You hit the string with a stick.

These women are dancing at a type of festival called a carnival.

Carnival dancers often wear amazingly spectacular costumes.

KOREA

Make this song sound very smooth. The tune also sounds good played on a violin, with a cello playing the notes in the left-hand piano part. The accompaniment is a simplified version of the tune.

Arirang

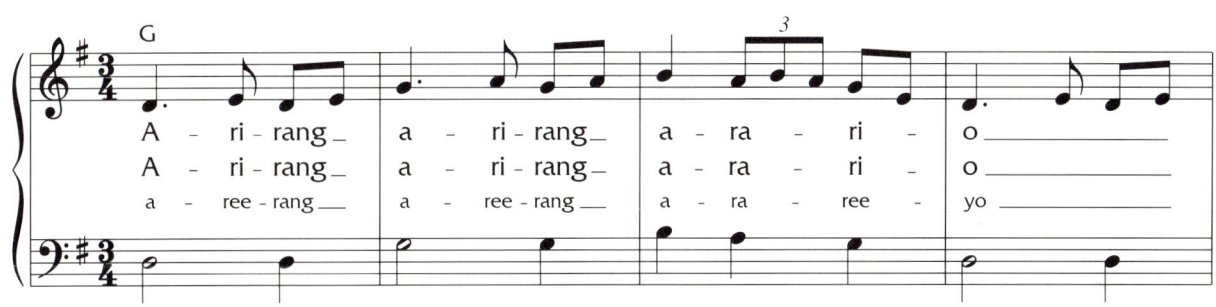

A - ri - rang — a - ri - rang — a - ra - ri - o ——
A - ri - rang — a - ri - rang — a - ra - ri - o ——
a - ree - rang — a - ree - rang — a - ra - ree - yo ——

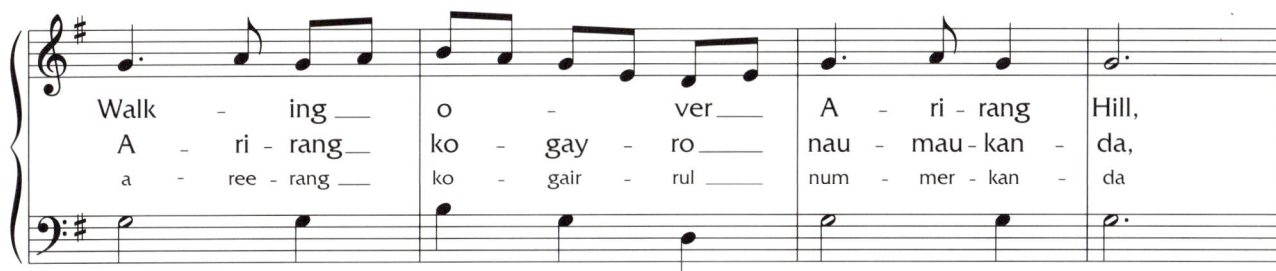

Walk - ing — o - ver — A - ri - rang Hill,
A - ri - rang — ko - gay - ro — nau - mau - kan - da,
a - ree - rang — ko - gair - rul — num - mer - kan - da

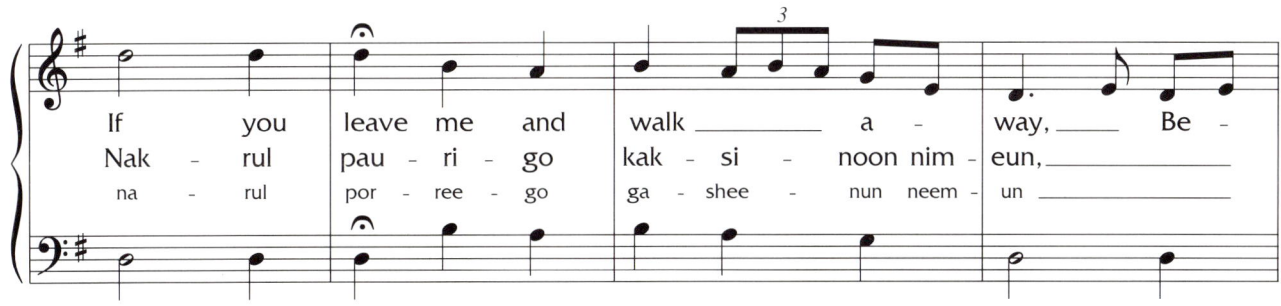

If you leave me and walk — a - way, — Be -
Nak - rul pau - ri - go kak - si - noon nim - eun,
na - rul por - ree - go ga - shee - nun neem - un

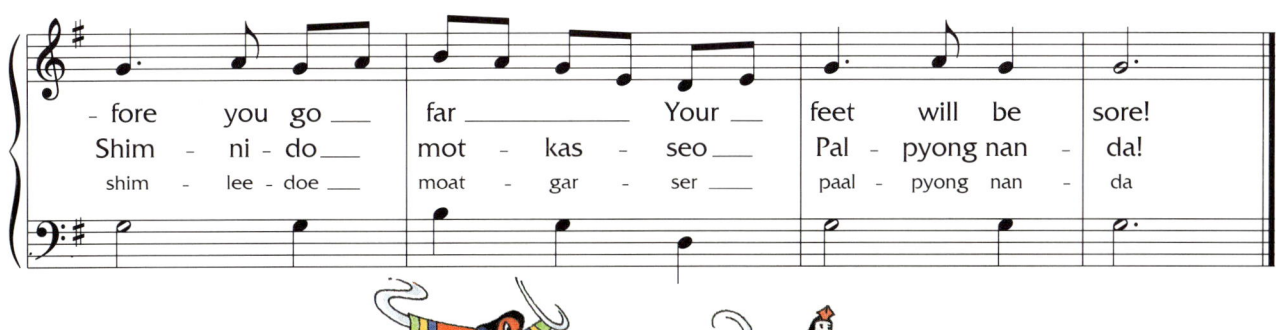

- fore you go — far — Your — feet will be sore!
Shim - ni - do — mot - kas - seo — Pal - pyong nan - da!
shim - lee - doe — moat - gar - ser — paal - pyong nan - da

MEXICO

The first eight measures of music below are a chorus. Sing them with the words shown in the music after each verse. Count the rhythm very carefully. You could ask someone to play a drum, a tambourine or maracas in the rhythm of the left-hand piano part.

The little beetle: *La cucaracha*

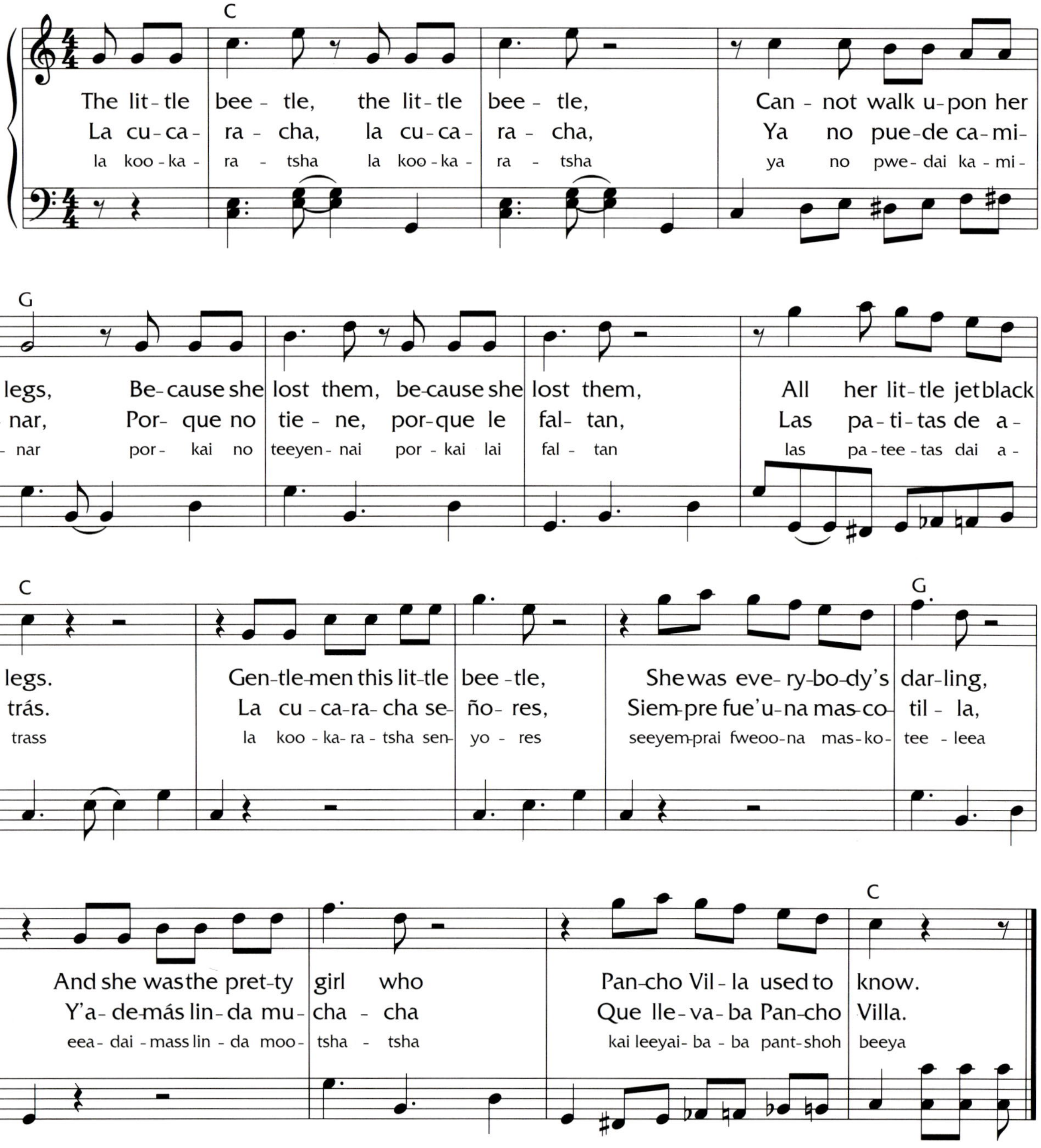

The lit-tle bee-tle, the lit-tle bee-tle, Can-not walk u-pon her legs, Be-cause she lost them, be-cause she lost them, All her lit-tle jet black legs. Gen-tle-men this lit-tle bee-tle, She was eve-ry-bo-dy's dar-ling, And she was the pret-ty girl who Pan-cho Vil-la used to know.

La cu-ca-ra-cha, la cu-ca-ra-cha, Ya no pue-de ca-mi-nar, Por-que no tie-ne, por-que le fal-tan, Las pa-ti-tas de a-trás. La cu-ca-ra-cha se-ño-res, Siem-pre fue'u-na mas-co-til-la, Y'a-de-más lin-da mu-cha-cha Que lle-va-ba Pan-cho Villa.

la koo-ka-ra-tsha la koo-ka-ra-tsha ya no pwe-dai ka-mi-nar por-kai no teeyen-nai por-kai lai fal-tan las pa-tee-tas dai a-trass la koo-ka-ra-tsha sen-yo-res seeyem-prai fweoo-na mas-ko-tee-leea eea-dai-mass lin-da moo-tsha-tsha kai leeyai-ba-ba pant-shoh beeya

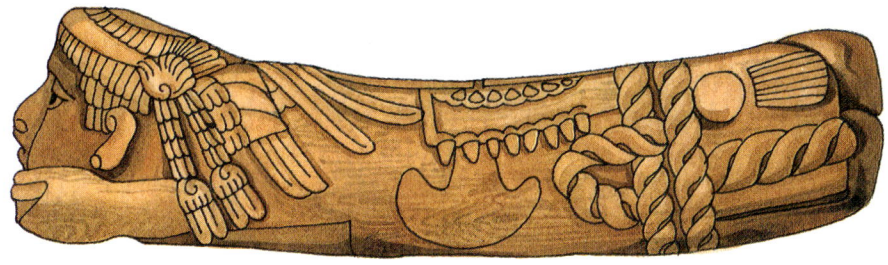

This wooden instrument is hollow inside. You hit it like a drum.

When a man admires a woman
But the woman doesn't like him,
It's the same as if a bald man
Finds a comb upon the street.

Cuando uno quiere a una
kwan-doe oo-no keeai-reya oo-na
Y esta una no lo quiere,
eeyess-ta oo-na no lo keeai-rai
Es lo mismo que si un calvo
ess lo meess-mo kessee oon kal-bo
En la calle encuentra un peine.
en la ka-lyahen-kwen-traoon peynyai

Mexico is full of women
Who are beautiful like flowers
And they speak so very sweetly
That they charm you with their love.

Las muchachas mexicanas
lass moo-tsha-tshass mai-hih-ka-nass
Son lindas como una flor
son leen-dass ko-mohoo-na flor
Y hablan tan dulcemente
ee a-blan tan dool-sai-men-tai
Que encantan de amor.
kai en-kan-tan dai a-mor

Horns are often used for signaling because their sound travels over long distances.

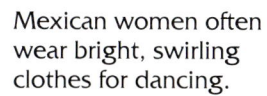

Mexican women often wear bright, swirling clothes for dancing.

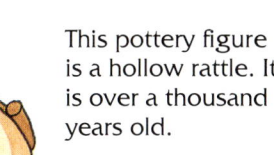

This pottery figure is a hollow rattle. It is over a thousand years old.

This man is playing a Mexican guitar, which is much larger than an ordinary guitar.

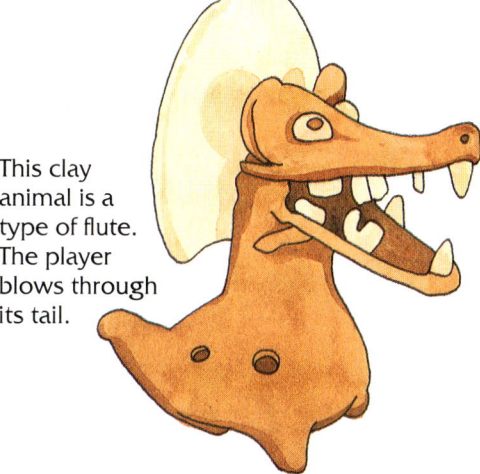

This clay animal is a type of flute. The player blows through its tail.

IRELAND

Make the dotted rhythms in measures 2, 4 and 6 sound very lively when you sing them. This tune will also sound good played on the recorder, flute or violin, with quick, repeated guitar strums for the accompaniment.

Cut the loaf

When I was young I had no sense, I bought a wee fid-dle for

eigh-teen pence, And all the tune that I could play was cut the loaf and ate a-way.

This instrument is an Irish harp, sometimes called a Celtic harp.

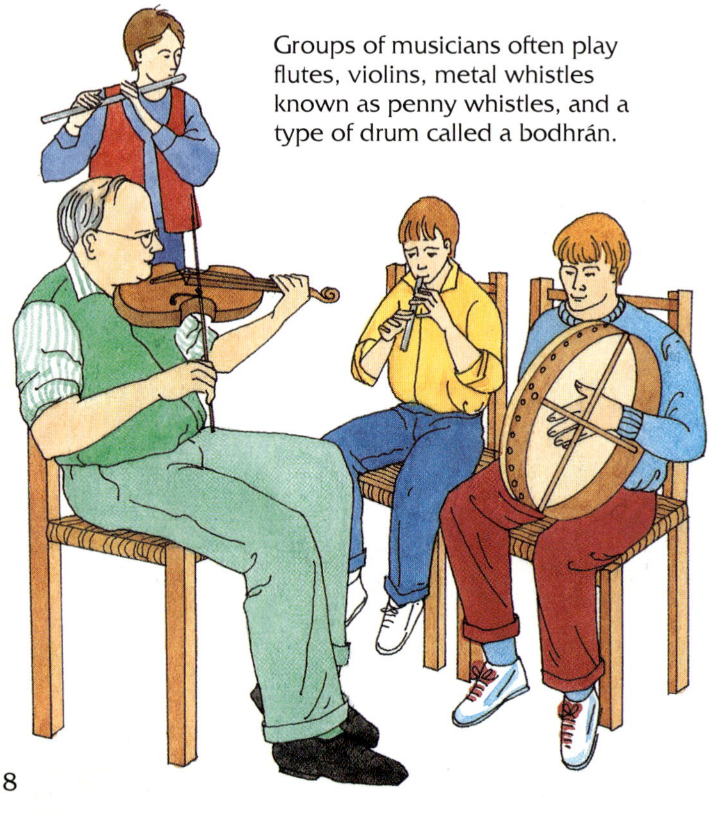

Groups of musicians often play flutes, violins, metal whistles known as penny whistles, and a type of drum called a bodhrán.

ISRAEL

This song has a very strong rhythm. You could stamp your feet on the beats as you sing. Make the piano accompaniment sound heavy and accented. Start the song fairly slowly, but get gradually faster in the last six measures.

Let's all rejoice: *Hava nagila*

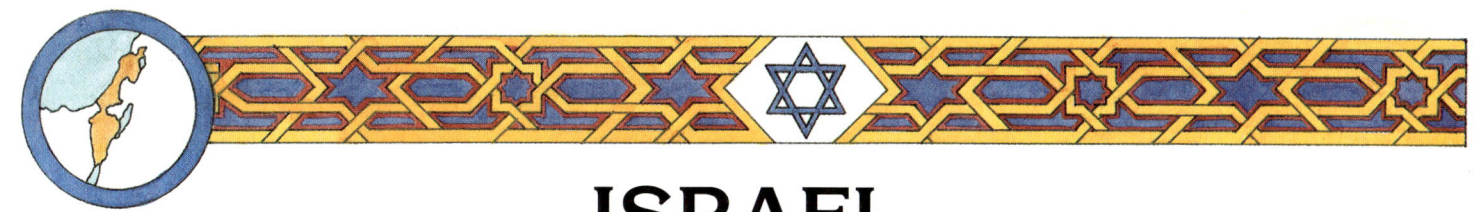

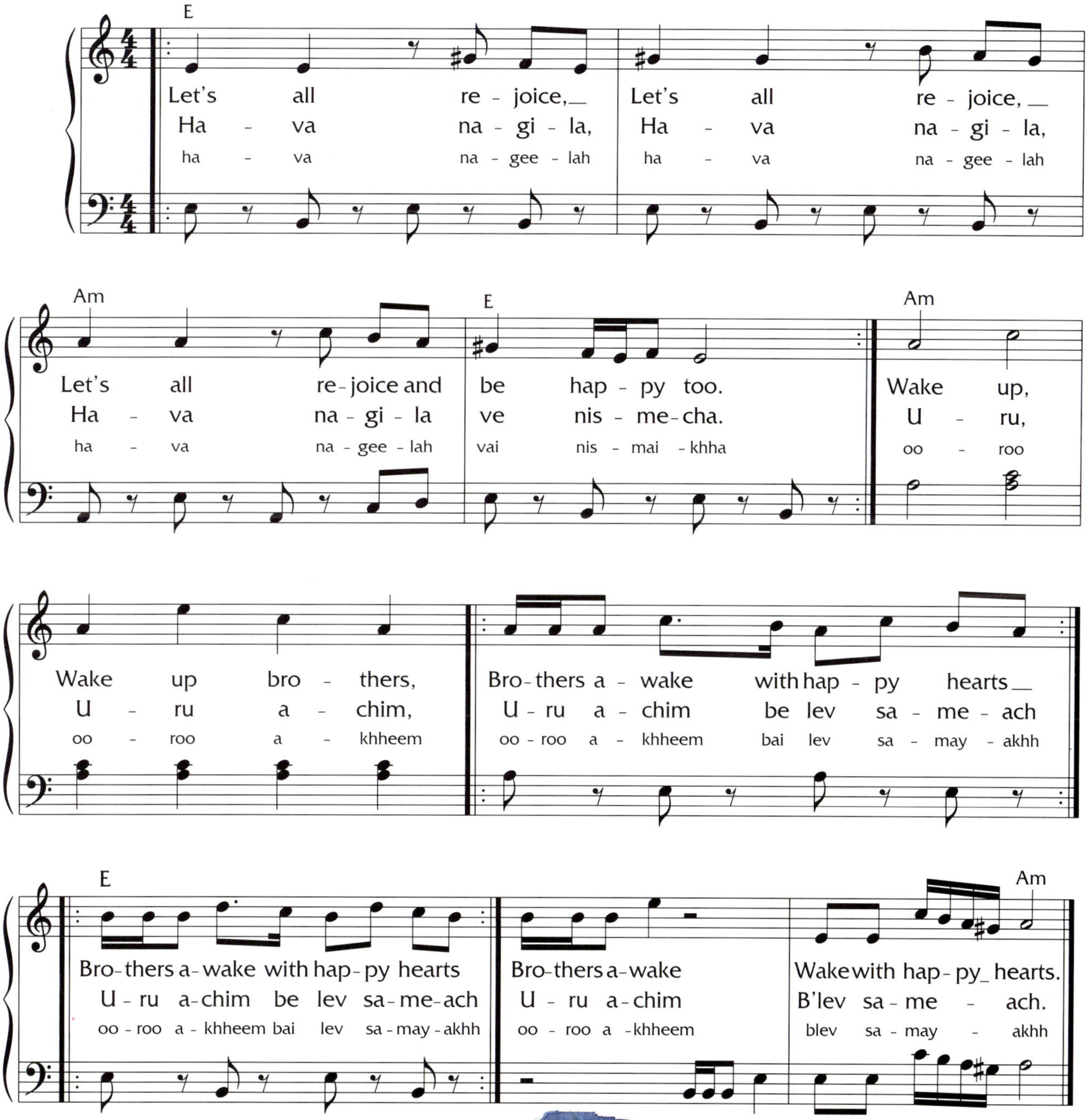

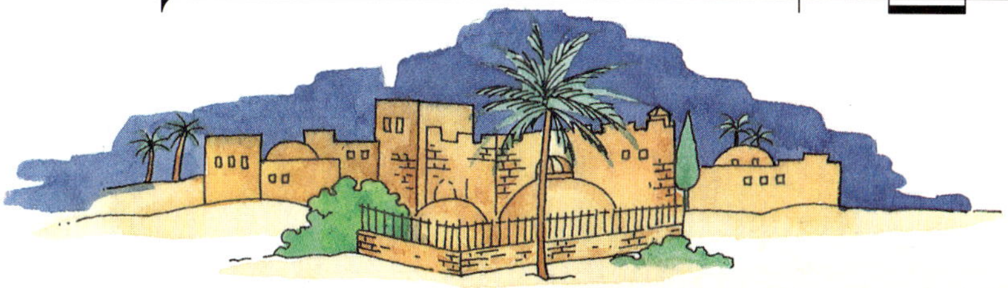

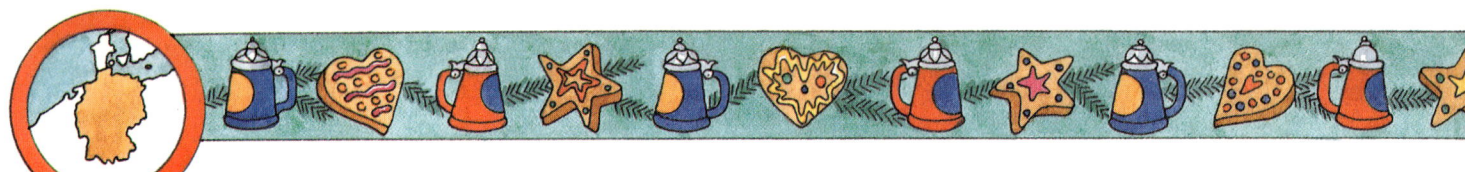

GERMANY

At the end of the fourth line of this song, you sing the first two lines of the music again, but this time to different words. You can see these extra words for this last part of the song on the opposite page.

Little Hans: *Hänschen klein*

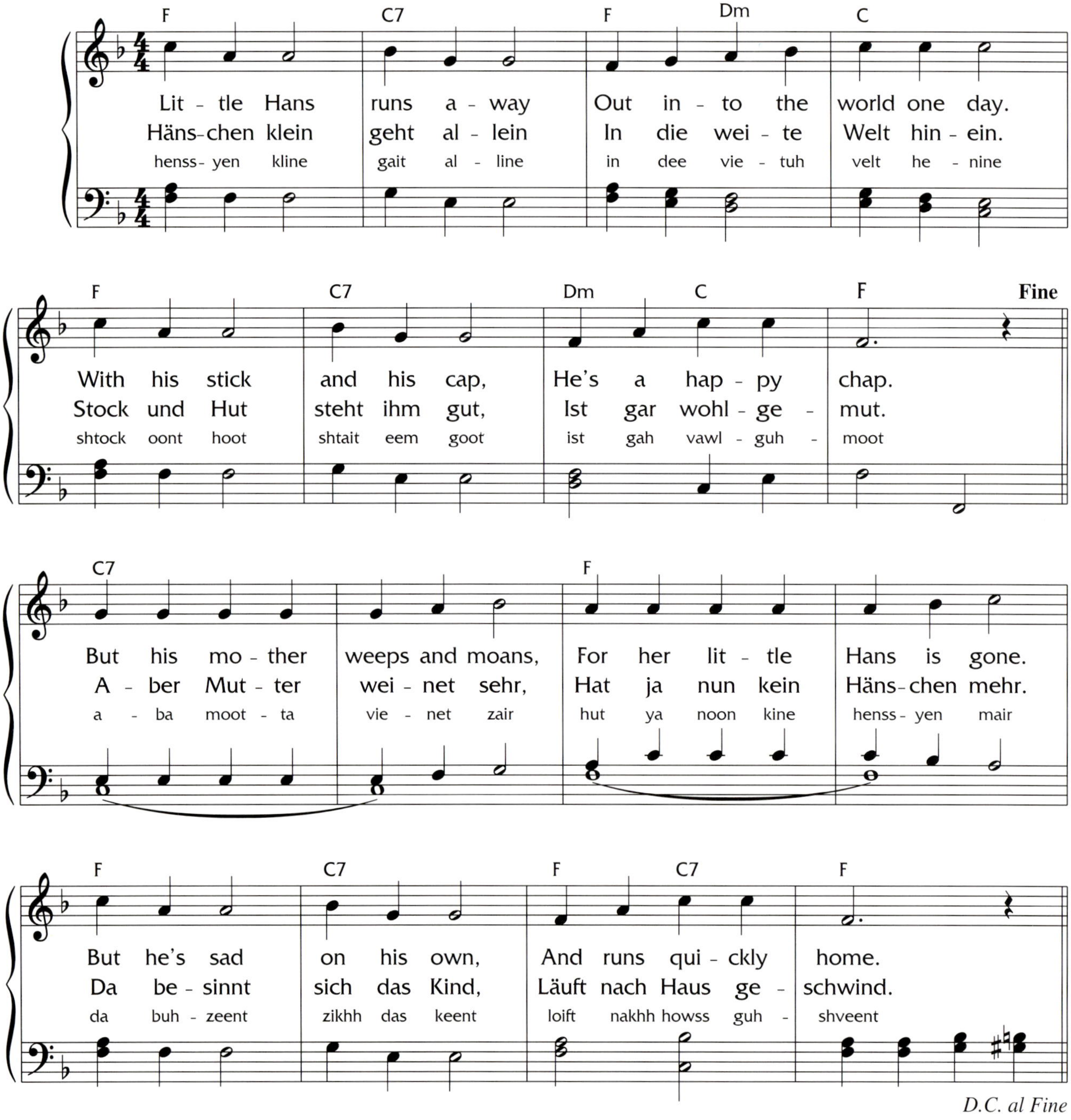
F C7 F Dm C
Lit - tle Hans runs a - way Out in - to the world one day.
Häns-chen klein geht al - lein In die wei - te Welt hin - ein.
henss- yen kline gait al - line in dee vie - tuh velt he - nine
F C7 Dm C F Fine
With his stick and his cap, He's a hap - py chap.
Stock und Hut steht ihm gut, Ist gar wohl - ge - mut.
shtock oont hoot shtait eem goot ist gah vawl - guh - moot
C7 F
But his mo - ther weeps and moans, For her lit - tle Hans is gone.
A - ber Mut - ter wei - net sehr, Hat ja nun kein Häns-chen mehr.
a - ba moot - ta vie - net zair hut ya noon kine henss- yen mair
F C7 F C7 F
But he's sad on his own, And runs qui - ckly home.
Da be - sinnt sich das Kind, Läuft nach Haus ge - schwind.
da buh - zeent zikhh das keent loift nakhh howss guh - shveent
D.C. al Fine

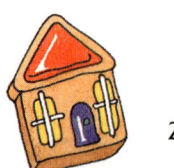

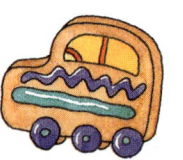

This is a jew's harp. It is made of silver. You hold it between your lips and pluck the flexible part with a finger.

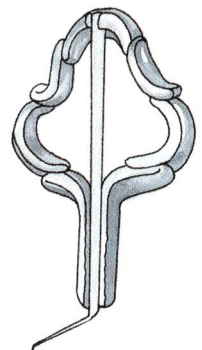

The alphorn is a long wooden trumpet played in the mountains. The sound can be heard a very long way away.

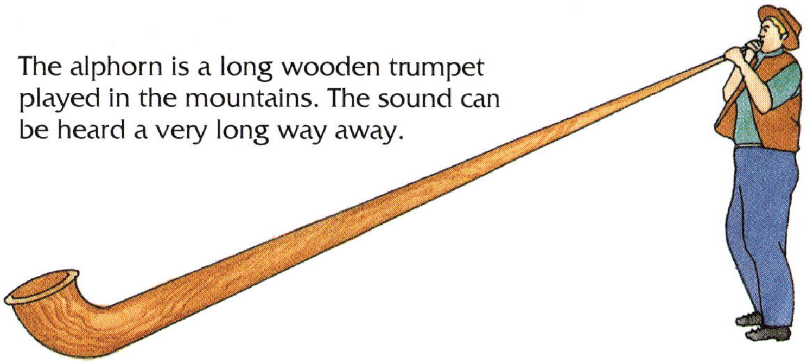

Here I am, dear mama,
Little Hans shouts tra-la-la,
I won't go off to hide,
I'll stay at your side.

Lieb' Mama, ich bin da,
leep ma-ma ikhh bin da
Ruft das Hänschen trallala,
rooft das henss-yen tra-la-la
Geh' nicht mehr fort von hier,
gay nikhht mair fort fon here
Bleib jetzt immer bei dir.
blipe yetst im-ma by deer

This type of small organ is often used by street entertainers.

Street organs do not have keyboards. You turn a handle to make them play.

Many German musicians play trumpets, tubas, trombones and drums in bands.

CANADA

This song is popular in parts of Canada where people speak French. The words originally came from France, but the tune is Canadian. Play the piano accompaniment very smoothly. The last two measures are a chorus. Sing them with the same words after each verse.

The clear fountain: *A la claire fontaine*

One day when I was wal-king | I found a foun-tain clear, | I saw the love-ly wa-ter,
A la clai-re fon-tai-ne M'en al-lant pro-me-ner, J'ai trou-vé l'eau si bel-le
a la klai-ruh fon-ten-nuh mon-na-lon prom-muh-nai jai troo-vai lo see bel-luh

So I went swim-ming here. | I've loved you for a long time, | I'll ne-ver for-get you.
Que je m'y suis bai-gné. Il y a long-temps que je t'ai-me, Ja-mais je ne t'ou-blie-rai.
kuh juh mee swee ben-yai eel-eea lon-ton kuh juh tai-muh ja-mai juh nuh too-blee-rai

I dried myself beneath
The leaves of an old oak tree,
Up on the highest branch
A nightingale sang to me.

Sous les feuilles d'un chêne
soo lai fur-yuh dun shen-nuh
Je me suis fait sécher,
juh muh swee fai sai-shai
Sur la plus haute branche
sewr la plew aw-tuh bron-shuh
Le rossignol chantait.
luh ro-see-neeol shon-tai

Up on the highest branch
A nightingale sang to me,
Sing, nightingale, sing,
Sing with a happy heart.

Sur la plus haute branche
sewr la plew aw-tuh bron-shuh
Le rossignol chantait,
luh ro-see-neeol shon-tai
Chante, rossignol, chante,
shon-tuh ro-see-neeol shon-tuh
Toi qui as le coeur gai.
twa kee a luh kur gai

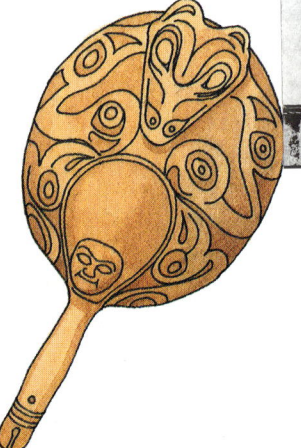

This drum has a handle. The player hits the wooden rim with a stick.

Both these carved wooden instruments are rattles.

22

JAVA

This is a singing game. One player is the serpent. The rest link up in a line. The serpent has to try to catch the person at the back, who is the food. The other players have to twist and turn the line to stop the serpent from catching the food.

Snaky serpent song: *Ular naga*

See the sna-ky ser-pent slide, he is ve-ry long,
U - lar na - ga pan-jang-nya bu - kan ke - pa - lang,
oo - lar na - ga pan - jang - nya boo - kan kuh - pa - lang

Here and there and ev-ery-where he sli-thers on and on, He is al-ways look-ing for a
Men - ja - lar - ja-lar se - la - lu ki - an ke-ma-ri, Um-pan yang le - zat i - tu-lah
muhn - ja - lar - ja-lar suh - la - loo kee-an kuh-ma-ree um - pan yang luh - zat ee - too-lah

ta - sty snack, Here it is, right here, hid - den at the back.
yang di - ca - ri, I - ni di - a - nya yang ter - be - la - kang.
yang dee - cha - ree ee - nee dee - a - nya yang tuhr - buh - la - kang

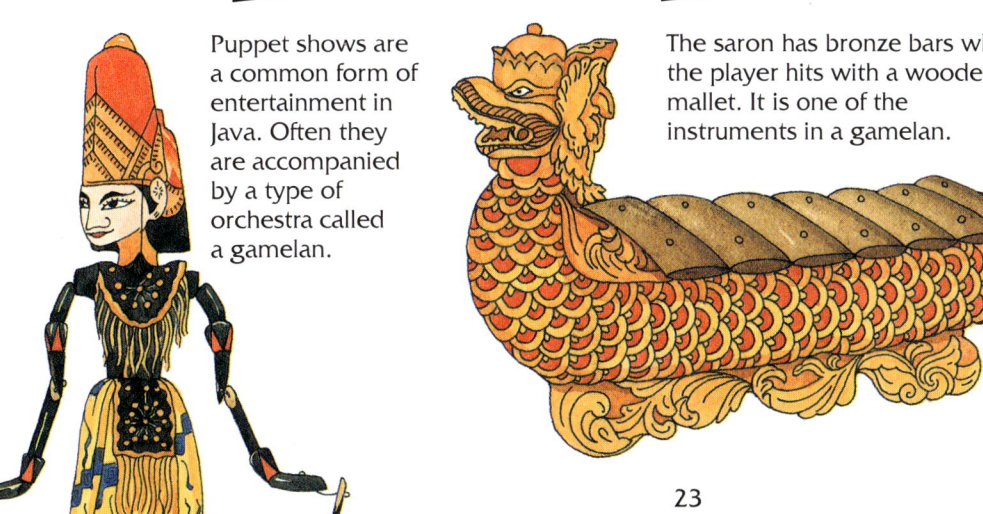

Puppet shows are a common form of entertainment in Java. Often they are accompanied by a type of orchestra called a gamelan.

The saron has bronze bars which the player hits with a wooden mallet. It is one of the instruments in a gamelan.

23

SCOTLAND

Sing this song at a steady speed. The repeated Cs in the left-hand piano part are called a drone. They sound a bit like the drone notes made by bagpipes. These notes would sound good played on other instruments as well, such as a cello, to make them stronger.

O where, tell me where

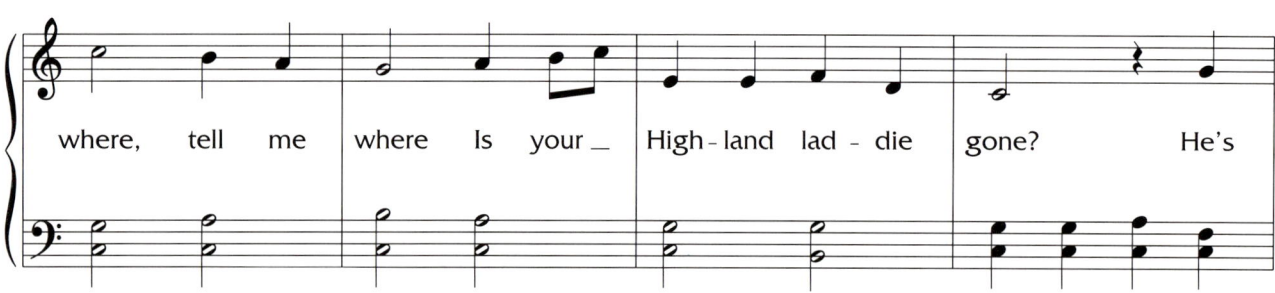
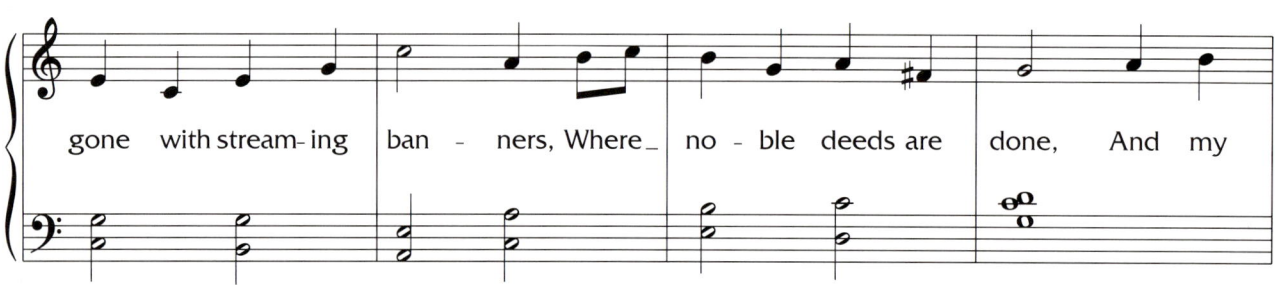
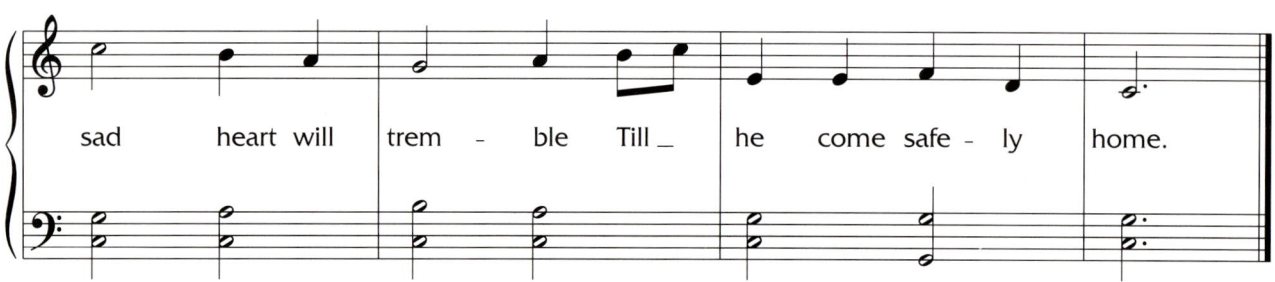

Bagpipes are often played in Scottish bands.

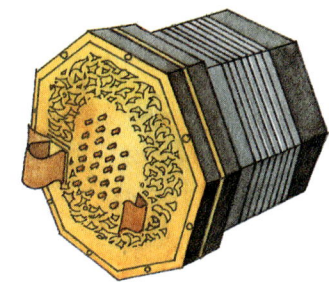

This is a concertina. You hold a handle at each end and squeeze it in and out to play.

O what, tell me what
Does your Highland laddie wear?
O what, tell me what
Does your Highland laddie wear?
A bonnet with a plume,
The gallant badge of war,
And a plaid on the breast
That yet shall wear a star.

Suppose, ah suppose
That some cruel, cruel wound
Should pierce your laddie,
And all your hopes confound?
The pipe would play a march,
The banners round him fly,
And for king and country
With pleasure would he die.

The Highland fling is a lively, springing dance. It is often accompanied by bagpipes.

Drums are often played in military bands to accompany bagpipes. The player wears the drum slung on a strap or belt.

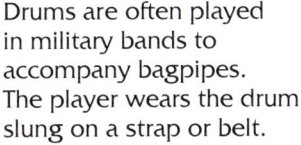

To play bagpipes, you blow air into a bag and use your arm to squeeze it out through the pipes. One of the pipes has finger holes so you can play different notes.

SPAIN

This song should sound very light. Make the piano chords bouncy without being loud or heavy. If you add in the guitar chords, play the bass note on the first beat of each measure, then the chord on the second beat. Leave a rest on the third beat.

Cuckoo, cuckoo: *Cucú, cucú*

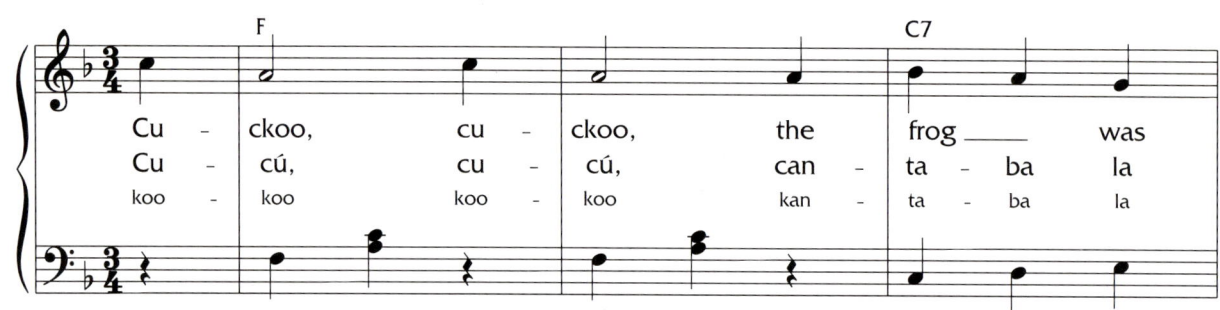
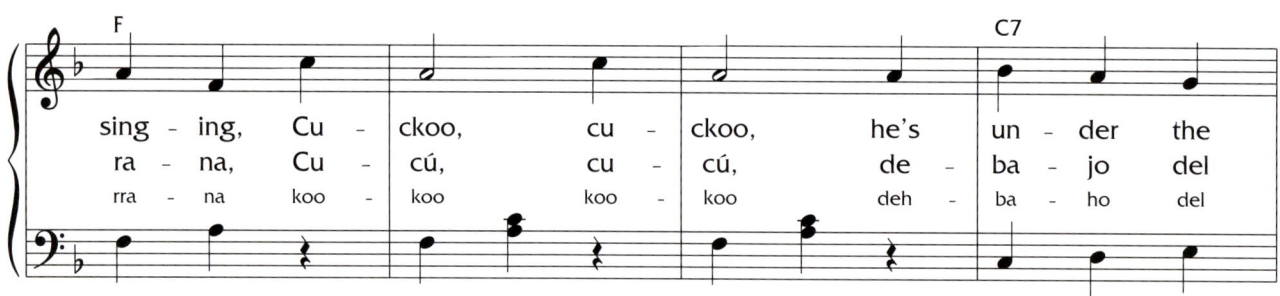
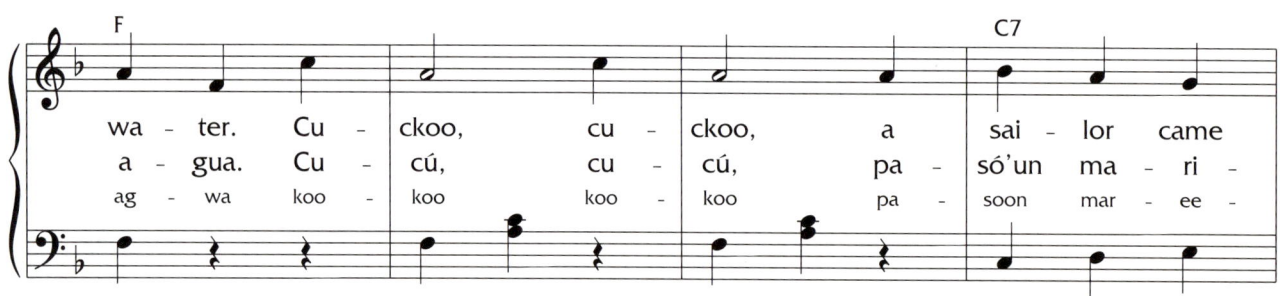
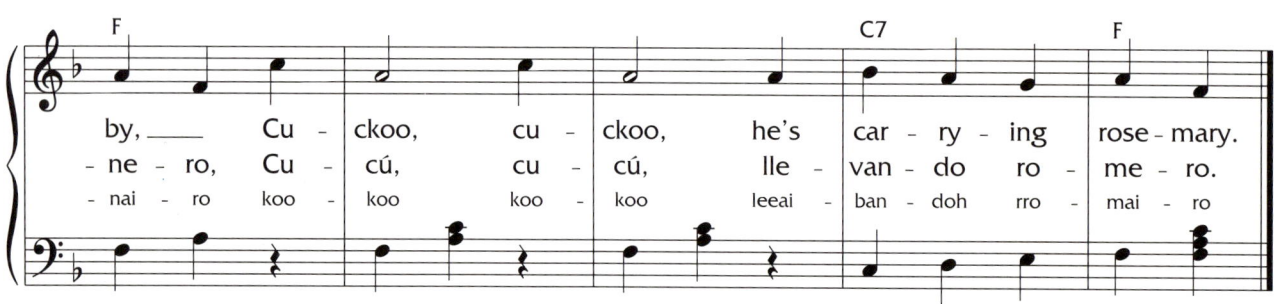

This early Spanish instrument is called a vihuela. It was played like a guitar.

These curved wooden disks are a type of percussion instrument called castanets. They make a clicking sound.

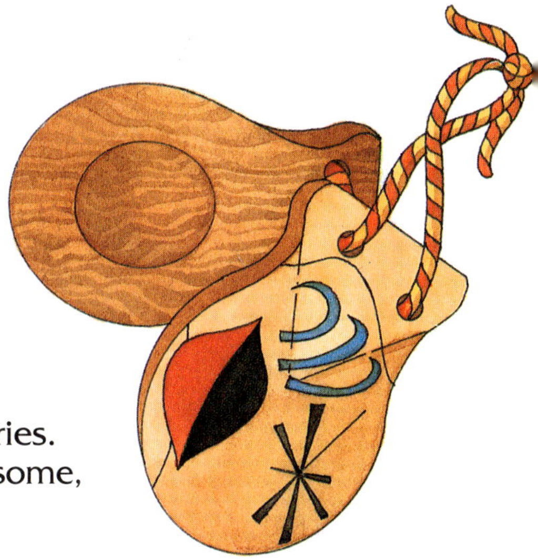

Cuckoo, cuckoo, a lady came by,
Cuckoo, cuckoo, she's carrying blackberries.
Cuckoo, cuckoo, she wouldn't give me some,
Cuckoo, cuckoo, I started to cry.

Cucú, cucú, pasó una señora,
koo-koo koo-koo pa-soo-na sen-yo-ra
Cucú, cucú, llevando unas moras.
koo-koo koo-koo leeai-ban-doeoo-nass maw-rass
Cucú, cucú, no me quiso dar,
koo-koo koo-koo noh mai kee-so dar
Cucú, cucú, me puse a llorar.
koo-koo koo-koo mai poo-seya leeor-rar

In Spain, there is a special type of music, song and dance called flamenco. You can see some flamenco dancers below.

Spanish dancers often click castanets in the palms of their hands while they are dancing.

Guitars are very important in flamenco music. They are often used as a solo instrument, as well as for accompanying singers and dancers.

Flamenco dancers stamp their heels in time with the music to make a strong rhythm.

WALES

Sing this song at a steady speed, not too fast. The first four measures of the piano accompaniment should sound very smooth. Take care that the left-hand chords in the second line do not sound heavy.

There is Daddy: *Dacw Dadi'n mynd i'r ffair*

There is Dad-dy go-ing to the fair To buy a cow to eat the grass To
Da-cw Da-di'n mynd i'r ffair I bry-nu buwch i fwy-ta gwair I
dah-coo dah-deen minnd eer fire ee bren-ee beookhh ee vooee-ta gwire ee

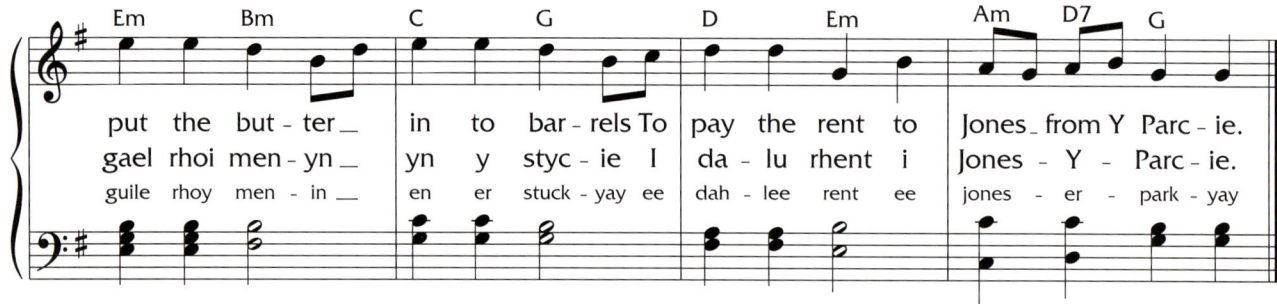

put the but-ter in to bar-rels To pay the rent to Jones from Y Parc-ie.
gael rhoi men-yn yn y styc-ie I da-lu rhent i Jones Y Parc-ie.
guile rhoy men-in en er stuck-yay ee dah-lee rent ee jones-er-park-yay

There is Daddy coming from the fair,
Oh let me take the cow to the field,
Tomorrow morning before you wake
I'll learn to milk her in the cowshed.

Dacw Dadi wedi dod yn ol
dah-coo dah-dee way-dee dawd en awl
Dadi gaf i fynd a'r fuwch i'r ddol
dah-dee garv ee vind are veookhh eer thawl
Bore fory cyn i chwi ddeffro
baw-ray vawree kin ee khhwee thay-fraw
Mi af i'r beudy i ddysgu sut i odro.
mee arv eer bay-dee ee the-sgee sit ee awd-raw

People playing violins often accompany dances.

These dancers are wearing wooden shoes called clogs which make a clacking sound when they hit the ground.

HOLLAND

You will probably recognize this tune, which is used for children's songs in many different countries. Make sure you sing the eighth notes carefully in measures 5 and 13. The first two measures of the music are an introduction.

Little Short Coat: *Altijd is Kortjakje ziek*

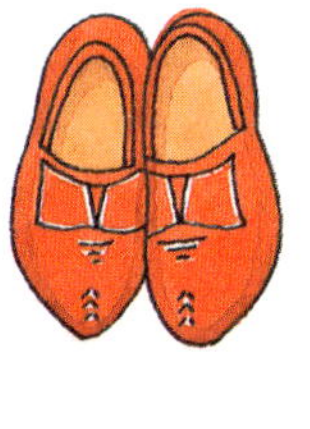

NEW ZEALAND

This type of song is often used by Maori people in New Zealand at the start of a concert. You need to count very carefully as you sing to make sure that you hold all the long notes for the correct length of time.

Greetings to you all!: *Tena ra koutou katoa!*

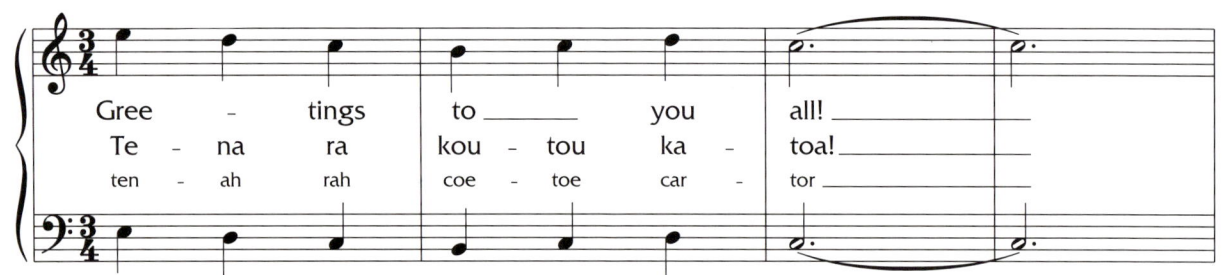

Gree - tings to you all!
Te - na ra kou - tou ka - toa!
ten - ah rah coe - toe car - tor

We say wel - come, Wel - come to all
Hae - re mai e nga, Hai - re mai e nga
ha-ai - rai my ai ngah ha-ai - rai my ai ngah

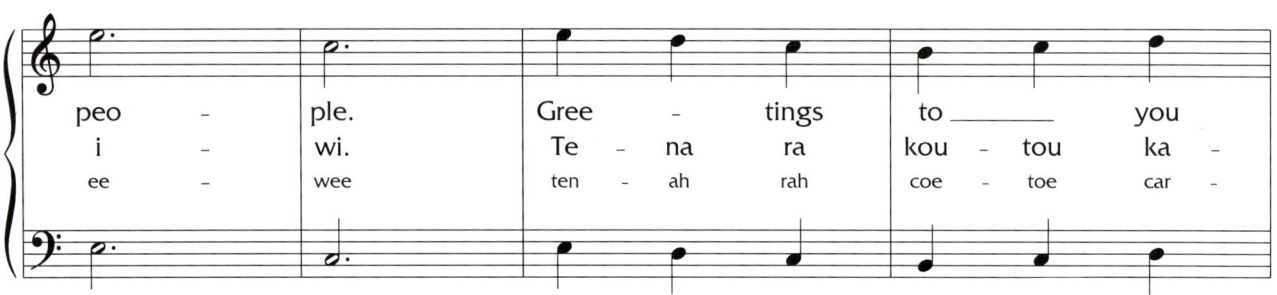

peo - ple. Gree - tings to you
i - wi. Te - na ra kou - tou ka -
ee - wee ten - ah rah coe - toe car -

This instrument is a type of trumpet. It has a hole at the right-hand end which you blow into, and a hole in the middle through which the sound escapes.

This whistle is called a nguru. It has two finger holes, one on each side, for playing different notes.

These instruments are a type of flute called a kooauau.

all! — Oh you peo - ple ga - thered
- toa! — E te i - wi hui to - nu
- tor — ai tai ee - wee hwee tor - noo

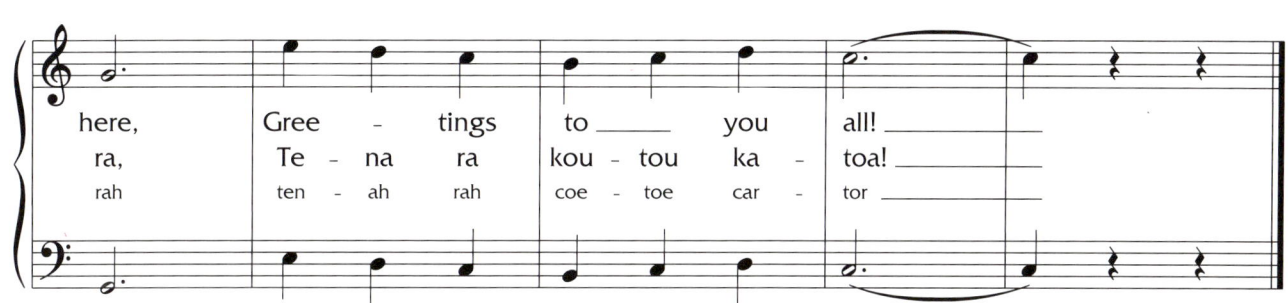

here, Gree - tings to you all! —
ra, Te na ra kou - tou ka - toa! —
rah ten - ah rah coe - toe car - tor

The woman on the left is doing a dance known as the poi. The dancers swing balls around on strings while they sing.

This Maori dance is called the haka. The dancers stamp, wave their arms and shout. It is often used for welcoming visitors. You might also see it at the start of a New Zealand rugby match.

Haka dancers often stick their tongues out and open their eyes very wide.

PHILIPPINES

This song is about a fishing trip. Bugaong and katambak are types of fish. One is nice to eat, the other is not. Sing the song fairly quickly, and make sure the piano chords do not sound heavy. You could sing it quietly the first time, then loudly when you repeat.

Fishing song: *Si nanay, si tatay*

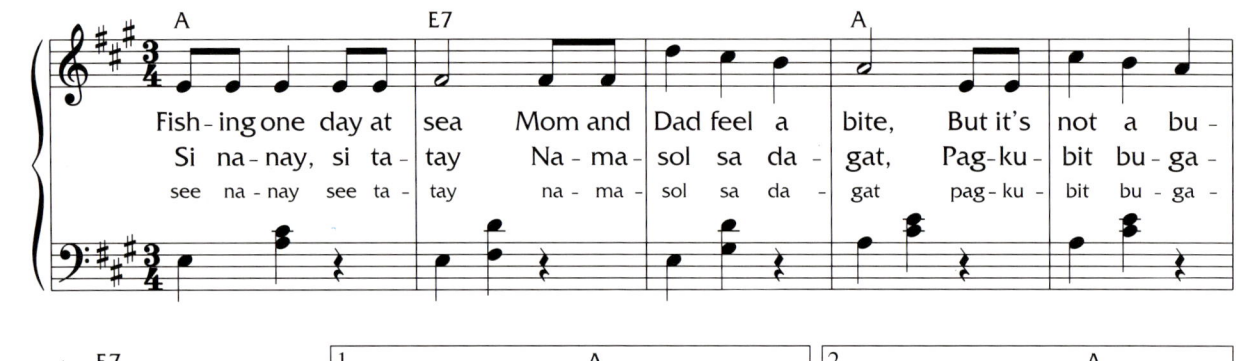

Fish-ing one day at sea | Mom and Dad feel a bite, | But it's not a bu-
Si na-nay, si ta-tay | Na-ma-sol sa da-gat, | Pag-ku-bit bu-ga-
see na-nay see ta-tay | na-ma-sol sa da-gat | pag-ku-bit bu-ga-

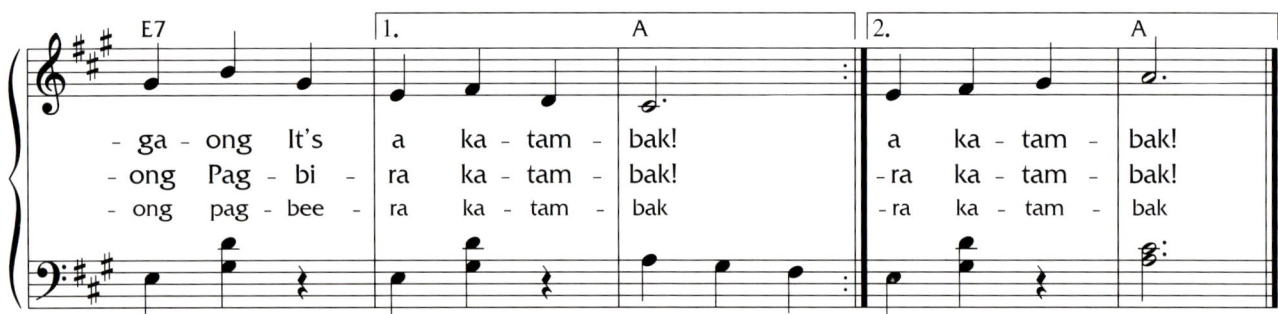

-ga-ong It's | a ka-tam-bak! ‖ a ka-tam-bak!
-ong Pag-bi-ra ka-tam-bak! | -ra ka-tam-bak!
-ong pag-bee-ra ka-tam-bak | -ra ka-tam-bak

This dance involves smooth, complicated movements with fans, while the dancers step between crisscrossed bamboo poles.

SOUTH AFRICA

Sing this song very gently and smoothly. The first two measures are an introduction. The melody could also be played on the recorder or violin, and the accompaniment on two cellos, one playing the top line and the other playing the bottom line.

Lord bless Africa: *Nkosi Sikelel' iAfrika*

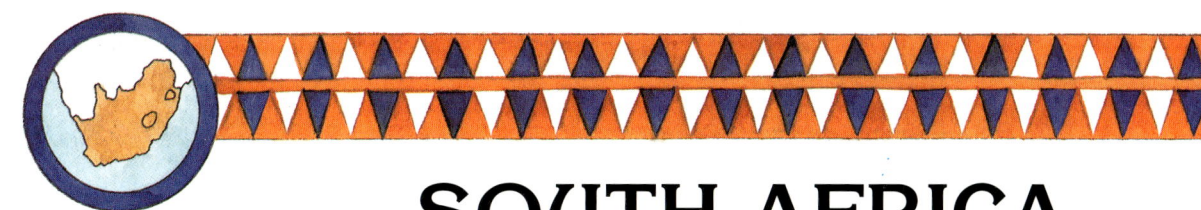

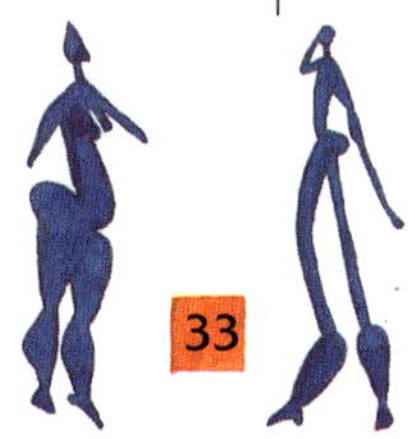

ENGLAND

This lullaby became popular over three hundred years ago. On the opposite page, you can see some instruments that were played at this time. The song should be very quiet. Make sure the chords in the piano accompaniment sound gentle.

Golden slumbers

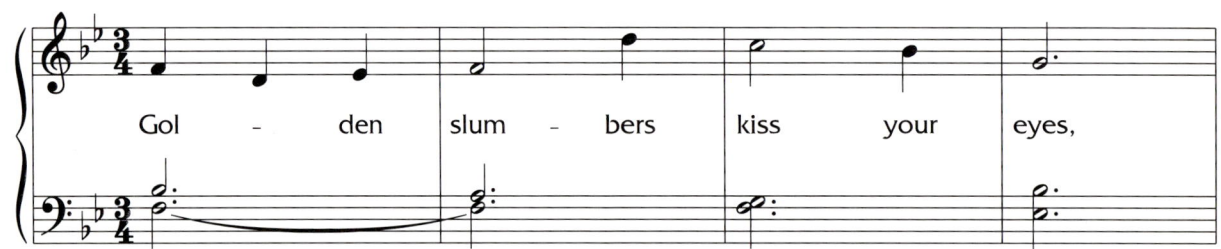

Gol - den slum - bers kiss your eyes,

Smiles a - wake you when you rise.

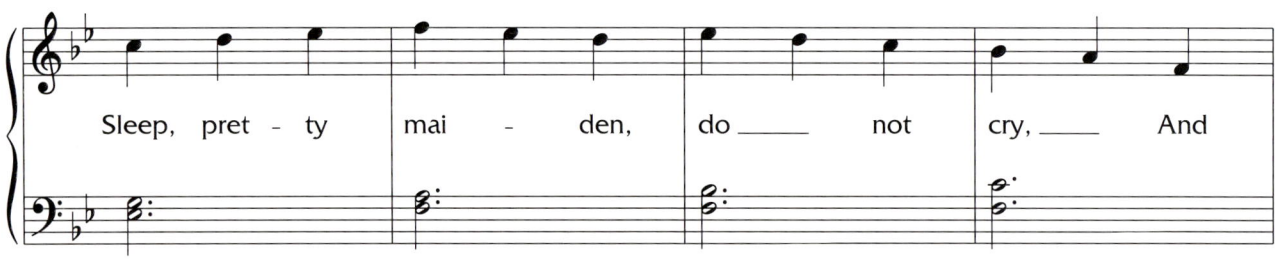

Sleep, pret - ty mai - den, do not cry, And

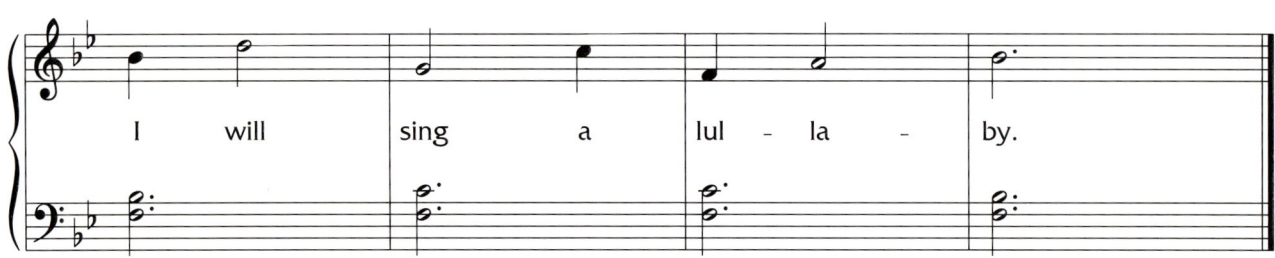

I will sing a lul - la - by.

This keyboard instrument is called a virginal. The strings were plucked inside by quills, small pieces of feather or leather.

A cittern had a flat back. The player plucked the strings with a small piece of wood or bone called a plectrum.

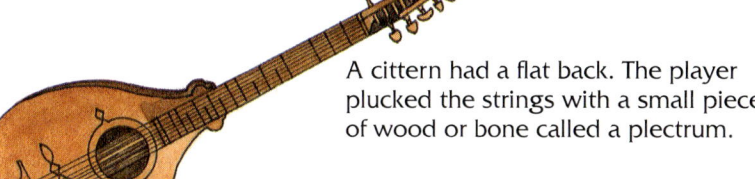

Care you know not, therefore sleep
While I o'er you watch do keep;
Sleep, pretty darling, do not cry,
And I will sing a lullaby.

Viols were stringed instruments which came in several different sizes. They were often played in groups.

This instrument, called a bass viol, was played with a bow. It was often used to play the bass line in a group.

Many people sang and played music with their friends. Learning an instrument was a very important part of education.

These people are playing a recorder and a stringed instrument called a lute.

Lutes were used for playing solos and accompanying. They had rounded bodies which were usually decorated with carving.

JAPAN

Learn the notes of this song very carefully, as they may sound a little unusual at first. Listen to the piano accompaniment too, as both hands play the same tune. Sing the song very smoothly and not too slowly.

Cherry blooms: *Sakura*

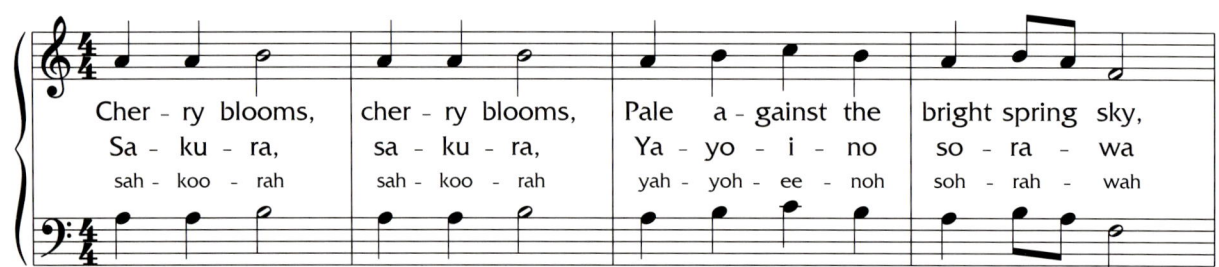

Cher - ry blooms, cher - ry blooms, Pale a - gainst the bright spring sky,
Sa - ku - ra, sa - ku - ra, Ya - yo - i - no so - ra - wa
sah - koo - rah   sah - koo - rah   yah - yoh - ee - noh   soh - rah - wah

Reach as far as we can see, Mi - sty blos - som in a cloud, Smell the per - fume
Mi - wa - ta - su ka - gi - ri Ka - su - mi - ka ku - mo - ka Ni - o - i - zo
mee - wah - tah - soo   kah - gee - ree   kah - soo - mee - kah   koo - moh - kah   nee - oh - ee - zoh

on the air. Come with me, come with me, Come and see, come and see.
i - zu - ru I - za - ya, i - za - ya, Mi - ni yu - kan.
ee - zoo - roo   ee - zah - yah   ee - zah - yah   mee - nee   you - kan

The koto has thirteen strings stretched over little bridges. The player presses the strings with one hand and plucks them with the other.

A shamisen is played a bit like a guitar. The player plucks the strings with a large piece of ivory.

HUNGARY

In this song, you sing the same words twice for each verse. The words for the extra verses are only written out once, so when you reach the fifth measure, repeat the words you have just sung to finish the verse.

When the spring comes: *Tavaszi szél vizet áraszt*

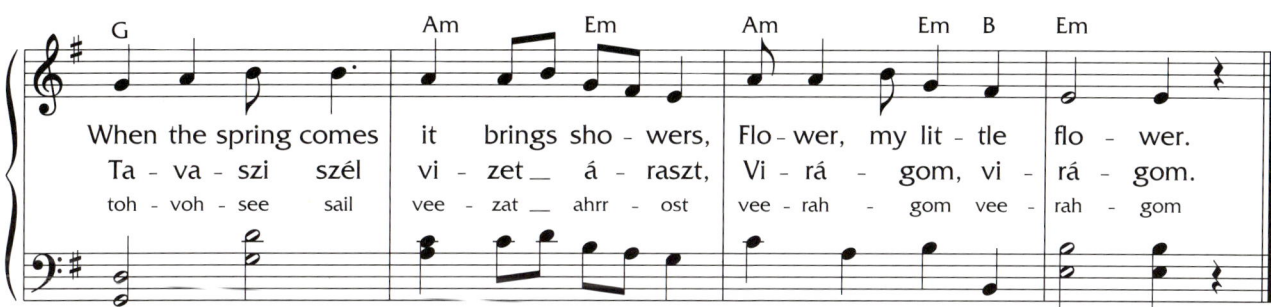

The instrument above is a nail violin. To play it, you rub a bow across the nails. The nails are different lengths, so they play different notes.

All the birds then find a partner,
Flower, little flower.

Minden madár társat választ,
min-den moh-darr tarr-shot vah-lost
Virágom, virágom.
vee-rah-gom vee-rah-gom

Please choose me to be your partner,
Sweetheart, little sweetheart.

Te engemet, s én tégedet,
teh an-geh-mat sh ain tai-ged-et
Virágom, virágom.
vee-rah-gom vee-rah-gom

The cimbalom is a Hungarian instrument which is played by hitting the strings with a pair of beaters.

This instrument is called a tárogató. It has a loud, harsh sound. You blow on two strips of cane at the top.

CHINA

In Chinese music, accompanying instruments often play the same tune as the singer, so the piano part below has the tune in both hands. The words in the last two measures imitate the sound of a drum. Sing them after the verse on the opposite page too.

Flower drum song: *Hua gu ge*

Gong on the left, drum on the right, Hol-ding a gong and drum
Zuo shou luo, you shou gu, Shou na zhe luo gu
zwo show lwo youw shou goo show nah juh lwo goo

I want to sing, But I can on-ly sing one song,
lai chang ge, Bie de ge-er wo ye bu hui chang,
lie chaang geh beeyer deh ge-er woh yeh boo hway chaang

I sing a-bout a flo-wer drum, I sing of a
Zhi hui chang ge feng yang ge, Feng la feng yang
jeh hway chaang geh feng yaang geh feng laa feng yaang

flo-wer drum. Der-er piaow der-er piaow piaow der-er piaow piaow piaow piaow.
ge-er lai. De-er piao de-er piao piao de-er piao piao piao piao.
ge-er lie der-er piaow der-er piaow piaow der-er piaow piaow piaow piaow

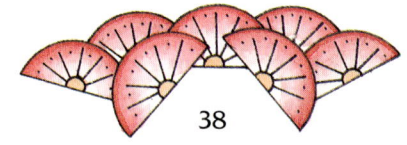

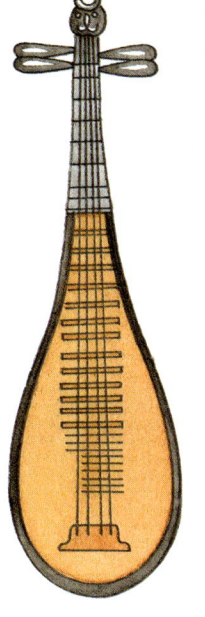

The pipa is a very old Chinese instrument. It has four strings and you hold it in your lap to play.

This instrument is called a gong chime. The gongs are different thicknesses to make different notes.

Fate brings me bitter luck,
I am not married to a good man,
Other men are luckier than he,
He just beats his flower drum,
He just beats his flower drum.

Wo ming ku, wo ming bo,
woh ming koo woh ming boh
Yi sheng yi shi jia bu zhe hao zhang fu,
yee sheng yee sheh jia boo juh how jaang foo
Ren jia zhang fu zuo guan zuo fu,
ren jia jaang foo zwo gwan zwo foo
Wo jia zhang fu ta hui da hua gu,
woh jia jaang foo tar hway dah hwa goo
Da da hua gu. Ao-ya-ai-hu-ya.
dah dah hwa goo ow-yaa-eye-hoo-yaa

Singers in Beijing opera wear lots of make-up and elaborate costumes. Beijing opera involves singing, acting, mime and acrobatics.

This singer is dressed in costume for a type of Chinese musical play known as Beijing opera.

These are bell chimes. Sometimes the bells are different sizes so they make different notes.

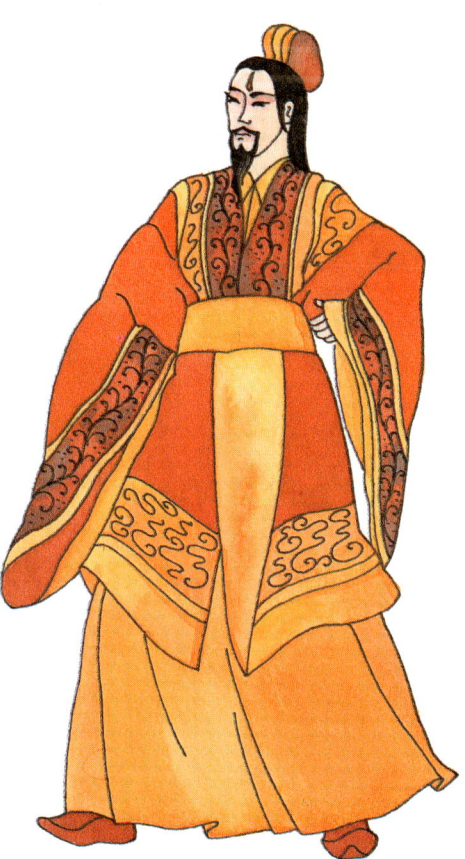

SAUDI ARABIA

This song is based on the call of a tradesman going from house to house trying to sell cloth. Make it sound very strong and lively. The left-hand piano part is similar to the tune but with some extra decorative notes.

Indian calico: *Bafta hindi*

Come and get your Indian fabric, Muslin and calico,
Bafta hindi, bafta hindi, Shash a-reed ya banat,
baf-ta hin-dee baf-ta hin-dee shash a-reed ya ba-nat

Open up your door oh girls, Or I'll climb through your window.
If-ta-hoo-li ya sa-ba-ya, Wal-la khosh min-li shib-bak.
if-ta-hoo-lee ya sa-ba-ya wal-la hoosh min-lee shib-bak

Young girl open up your door
For I've got some goods for you,
Silken garments, lovely curtains
And embroidery just for you.

Iftaheeli ya sabeya
if-ta-hee-lee ya sa-be-ya
Ândi bdaaa lisistat,
an-dee bdaah lis-sit-tat
Ândi harayer wi satayer
an-dee ha-ra-yerr wee sa-ta-yerr
Wi tantella lilbanat.
wee tan-tel-la lil-ba-nat

There are many kinds of dances in different parts of Saudi Arabia. Often they are accompanied by drums, to make a strong rhythm.

40

WEST INDIES

Tap the rhythm of this song before you sing it, counting very carefully. Then, when you sing, try to make it sound very relaxed, yet lively at the same time. You could also shake some maracas or a tambourine in time with the music.

Tinga Layo

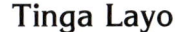

AUSTRALIA

A kookaburra is a type of bird. Sing this song fairly quickly, and make sure the chords in the piano accompaniment sound light and bouncy. The first four measures are an introduction. You could try tapping some claves to the rhythm of the tune.

Kookaburra

Koo - ka - bur - ra sits on the old gum tree, ____
Mer - ry mer - ry king of the bush is he. ____

These rattles are made from dried seed pods. The seeds are still inside, so they rattle when you shake the pod.

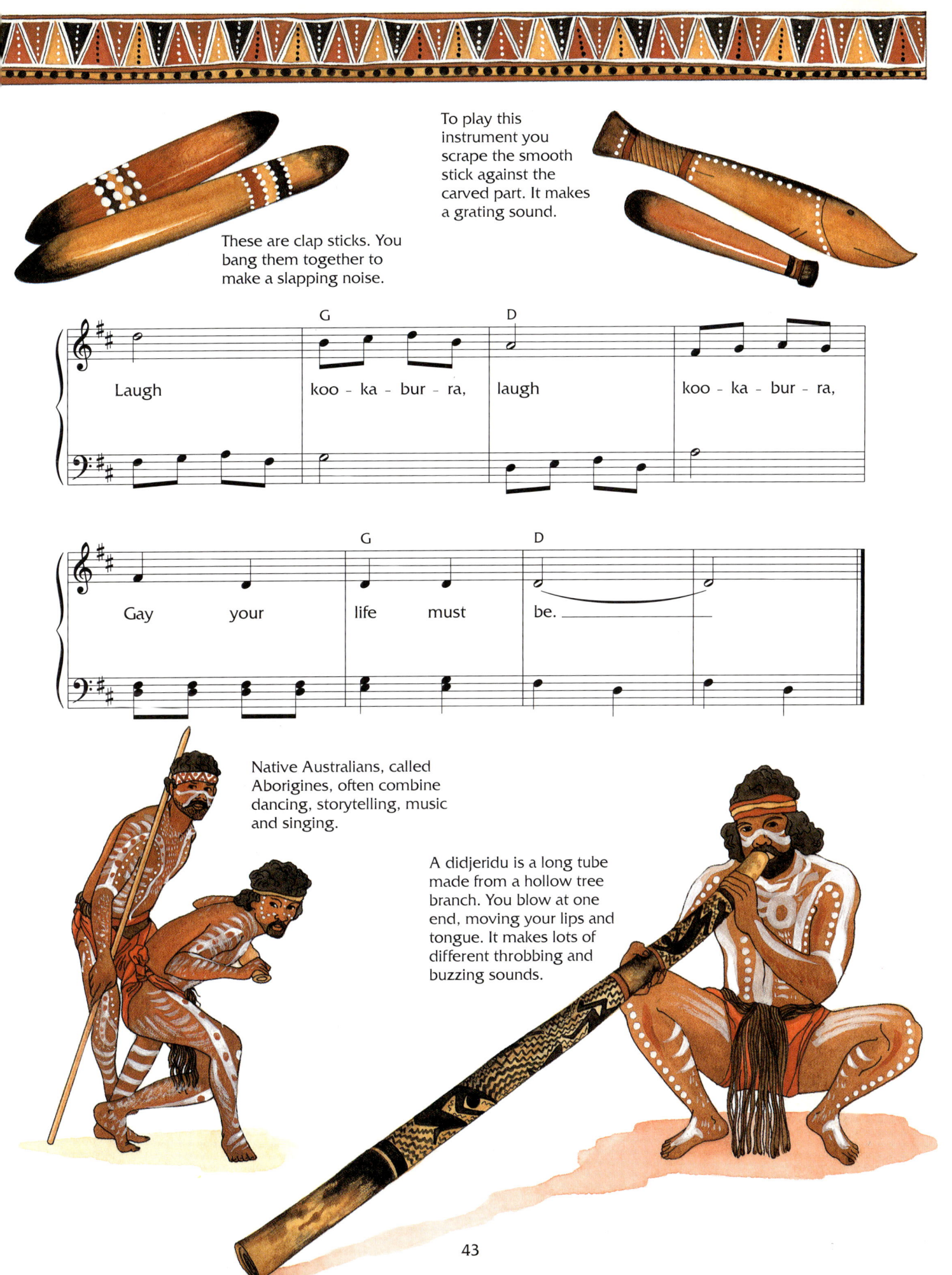

These are clap sticks. You bang them together to make a slapping noise.

To play this instrument you scrape the smooth stick against the carved part. It makes a grating sound.

Laugh koo-ka-bur-ra, laugh koo-ka-bur-ra, Gay your life must be.

Native Australians, called Aborigines, often combine dancing, storytelling, music and singing.

A didjeridu is a long tube made from a hollow tree branch. You blow at one end, moving your lips and tongue. It makes lots of different throbbing and buzzing sounds.

ITALY

This song is a lullaby. Sing it very quietly and smoothly. If you use a guitar, strum the chords slowly, or pick out single notes. Play in an eighth note rhythm, like the left-hand of the piano part, to make a gentle, lilting sound.

Go to sleep: *Ninna nanna*

| C | | Am | Dm |

Go to sleep now You are your Ma-ma's dar-ling.
Nin-na nan-na Coc-co-lo del-la Mam-ma.
neen-na nan-na kock-o-lo del-la ma-ma

| Dm7 | | G7 | C |

Go to sleep now You are your Dad-dy's love.
Nin-na nan-na Coc-co-lo del Pa-pà.
neen-na nan-na kock-o-lo del pa-pa

| C | | Am | Dm |

Go to sleep now You are your Ma-ma's dar-ling.
Nin-na nan-na Coc-co-lo del-la Mam-ma.
neen-na nan-na kock-o-lo del-la ma-ma

| Dm7 | | G7 | C |

Go to sleep now You are your Dad-dy's love.
Nin-na nan-na Coc-co-lo del Pa-pà.
neen-na nan-na kock-o-lo del pa-pa

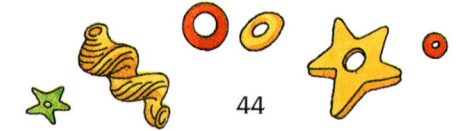

NIGERIA

Drums, rattles and other instruments for making rhythms are very important in Nigerian music. While you sing this song, you could bang a drum or clap your hands on the last one or two eighth beats of each measure.

On a farm I saw a bird: *Mo ri eye kan loko*

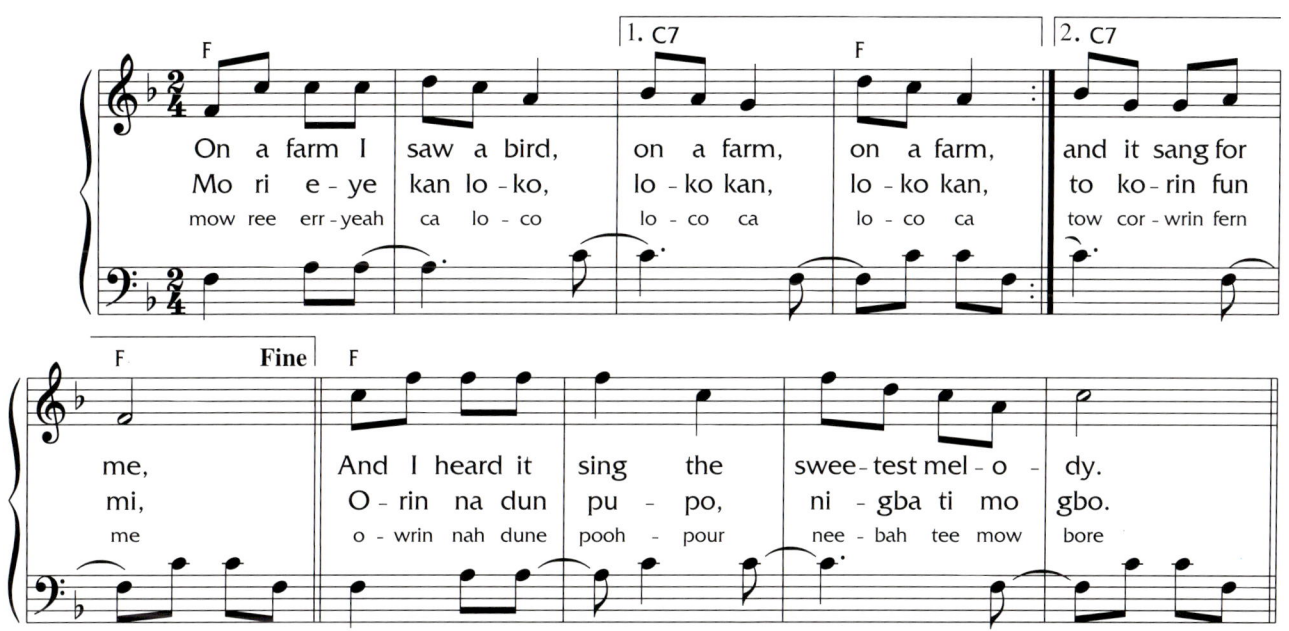

On a farm I saw a bird, on a farm, on a farm, and it sang for me, And I heard it sing the sweetest melody.
Mo ri eye kan lo-ko, lo-ko kan, lo-ko kan, to ko-rin fun mi, O-rin na dun pu-po, ni-gba ti mo gbo.
(mow ree err-yeah ca lo-co lo-co ca lo-co ca tow cor-wrin fern me o-wrin nah dune pooh-pour nee-bah tee mow bore)

D.C. al Fine

These people are playing guitars made from dried, hollow fruit skins.

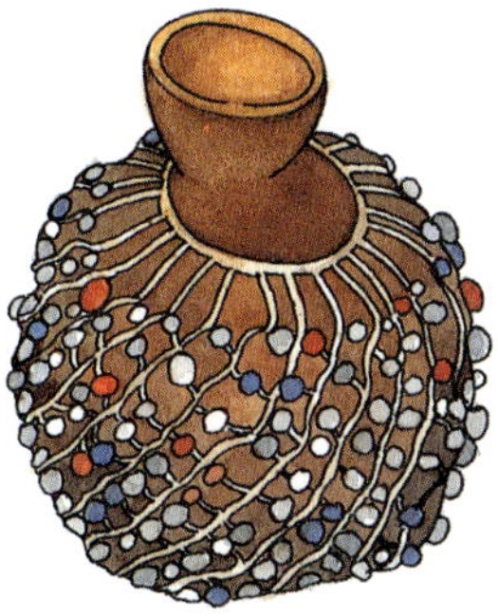

Talking drums have strings attached to the skins. The player squeezes the strings under his arm to make the drum play high or low notes.

This rattle is made from a dried fruit skin. It is covered with a net, threaded with beads. These rustle against the skin when you shake it.

45

PERU

Work out the rhythm of this song carefully before you start. Make sure the sixteenth note, eighth note, sixteenth note pattern (in measure 5 for example) is very clear. The guitar chords will sound good strummed in the rhythm of the left-hand piano part.

Please don't forget me: *Ama qonqawaychu*

Please don't for - get me / Wher - ev - er I go,
A - ma qon - qa - way - chu / May - ta ri - poq - tiy - pas,
a - mah gon - gah - waee - choo / maee - tah ree - poh - tee - pahs

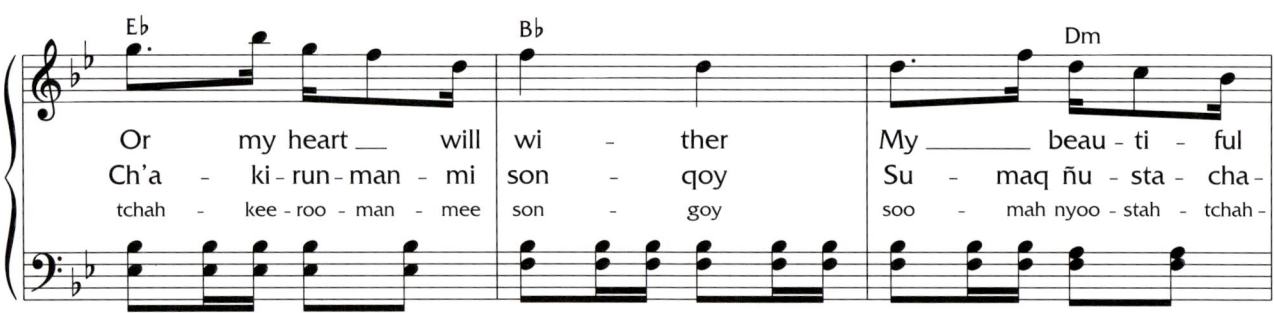

Or my heart will wi - ther / My beau - ti - ful
Ch'a - ki - run - man - mi son - qoy / Su - maq ñu - sta - cha -
tchah - kee - roo - man - mee son - goy / soo - mah nyoo - stah - tchah -

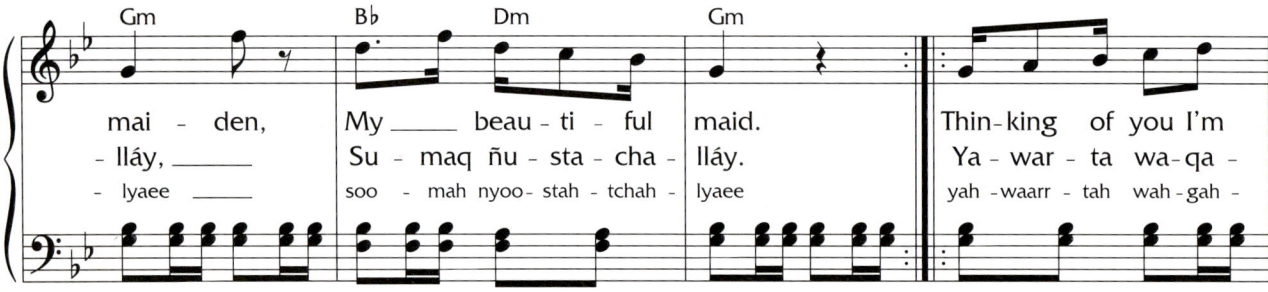

mai - den, / My beau - ti - ful maid. / Thin - king of you I'm
- lláy, / Su - maq ñu - sta - cha - lláy. / Ya - war - ta wa - qa -
- lyaee / soo - mah nyoo - stah - tchah - lyaee / yah - waarr - tah wah - gah -

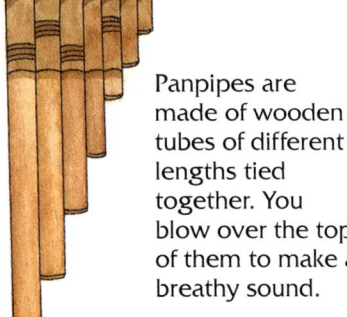

Panpipes are made of wooden tubes of different lengths tied together. You blow over the top of them to make a breathy sound.

Bands of musicians singing and playing panpipes, flutes and guitars are very popular in Peru.

INDEX OF COUNTRIES

Australia	42	Greece	7	Japan	36	Russia	8
Brazil	14	Holland	29	Java	23	Saudi Arabia	40
Canada	22	Hungary	37	Korea	15	Scotland	24
China	38	India	4	Mexico	16	South Africa	33
England	34	Ireland	18	New Zealand	30	Spain	26
Finland	10	Israel	19	Nigeria	45	USA	6
France	11	Italy	44	Peru	46	Wales	28
Germany	20	Jamaica	12	Philippines	32	West Indies	41

GUITAR CHORDS

The diagrams below show you how to play all the guitar chords used in this book. The vertical lines represent the strings (the lowest on the left) and the horizontal lines are the frets (the top thick line is the nut). The spots show you where to press the strings, and the numbers beneath tell you which left-hand fingers to use. An o above a string tells you to play it without using any left-hand fingers. An x means you don't play the string at all. A curved line tells you to press a finger across more than one string.

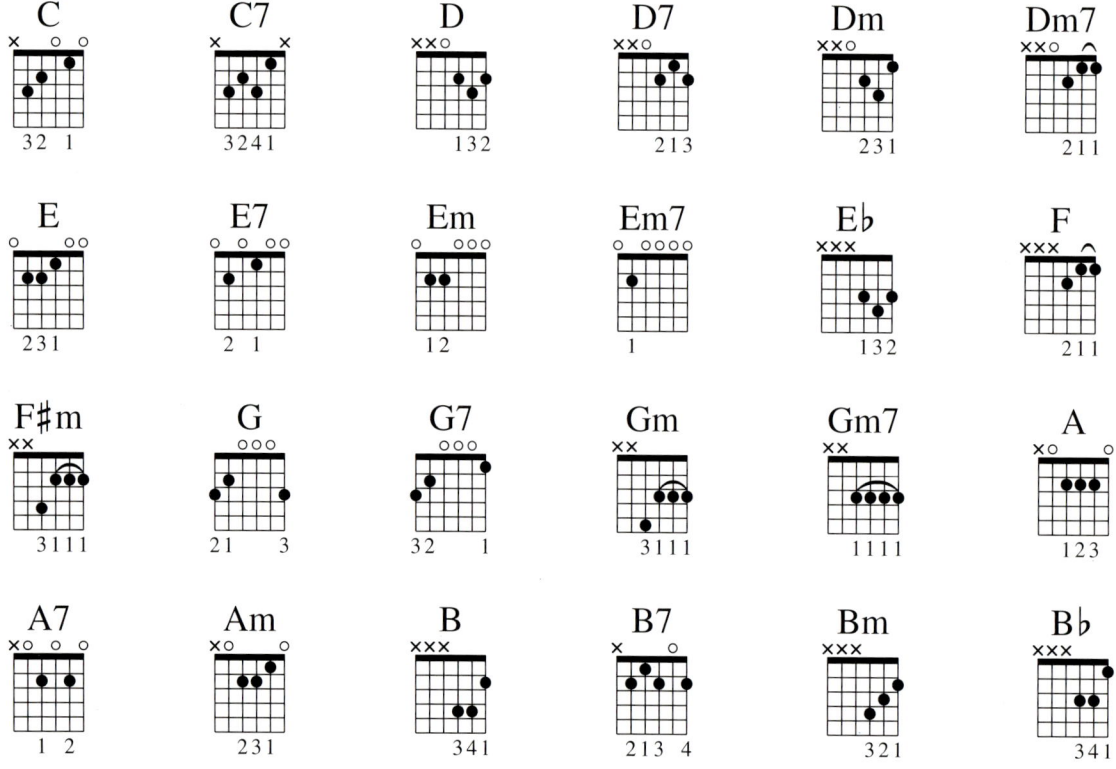

First published in 1995 by Usborne Publishing Ltd, Usborne House, 83-85 Saffron Hill, London EC1N 8RT. Copyright © 1995 Usborne Publishing Ltd. AE. First published in America March 1996.

The name Usborne and the device are Trade Marks of Usborne Publishing Ltd. All rights reserved. No part of this publication may be reproduced, stored in a retrieval system or transmitted in any form or by any means, electronic, mechanical, photocopying, recording or otherwise, without the prior permission of the publisher. Printed in Portugal.

Every effort has been made to trace the copyright owners of songs in this book. If any right has been omitted, the publishers offer their apologies and, following notification, will rectify this in any further editions.